DESIGNING AND MAKING STAGE COSTUMES

SILHOUETTES OF
COSTUME FROM THE 12th
TO THE 16th CENTURY

13th CENTURY

12th CENTURY

EARLY 16th CENTURY

LATE 15th CENTURY

14th CENTURY

15th CENTURY

EARLY 16th CENTURY

ELIZABETHAN

DESIGNING AND MAKING STAGE COSTUMES

MOTLEY

FOREWORD BY DAME PEGGY ASHCROFT

Revised edition edited and introduced
by Michael Mullin

THE HERBERT PRESS

First edition 1964

This revised edition first published in Great Britain 1992
by The Herbert Press Ltd, 46 Northchurch Road, London N1 4EJ

Set in Imprint

Printed and bound in Hong Kong by South China Printing
Company (1988) Ltd

A CIP catalogue record for this book is available from the British Library

ISBN 1-871569-44-3

The authors are grateful to all those designers who have been kind enough to allow their sketches to be reproduced in this book. They would also like to thank Professor Kathleen Campbell of George Mason University for assistance with the Select Bibliography.

Front cover illustration: Design for Elizabeth Taylor's costume worn at Michael Todd's birthday celebration, Madison Square Garden, New York, 1957

CONTENTS

FOREWORD

It was with great pleasure that I undertook to write a foreword to this book, in spite of the fact that I felt it was a task I might not be qualified to fulfil. But I have known 'the Motleys' throughout their career – indeed, I can boast that I was in their first production: John Gielgud's OUDS production of *Romeo and Juliet* in 1932 for which they designed the costumes. Soon after that they achieved a meteoric success in Gielgud's season at the New Theatre – *Richard of Bordeaux, Hamlet, Noah,* and *Romeo and Juliet* – and later, in 1937, at the Queens – *School for Scandal, The Three Sisters, Richard II* and *The Merchant of Venice.* The list of their successes is too many to enumerate, and anyway it is not necessary to remind the reader of their many productions and their variety. This is a book about the craft of theatre design and particularly that of designing and making costumes; and it is the Motleys' devotion to their craft, their complete mastery of it, allied to their very considerable talent, and, above all, their unswerving aim to serve and interpret the play and the producer's vision of it that are their great qualities.

Theatre design is, to my mind, an art quite on its own. Great painters such as Picasso, Derain and Benois have designed decor for ballets which remain part of one's vision of the ballet for ever. But I think theatre designers have to master more technical difficulties. They have to appreciate exactly what are the play's necessities, the producer's conception, the actors' problems; they are, in fact, servants of the theatre as are the actors. Perhaps for this reason the interpretative and essentially partner-like quality necessary for this work is often found at its highest in women. Certainly in our generation Motley (consisting of three women – Sophie Devine, Margaret Harris and Elizabeth Montgomery), Tanya Moiseiwitsch and Jocelyn Herbert are unsurpassed. Motley arrived early at the top and they stayed there through many years. They had a very individual style from the beginning, but it has never become set and their work has continually grown and developed and has embraced every variety of production.

In the later years of an artist's work, it is interesting to assess not only the quality and significance of what they have achieved, but also their influence on their contemporaries and successors. One of the most interesting features of the theatre in the 'thirties was the work of Gielgud at the New Theatre, and later at the Queens, and this made a profound change in the London theatre scene. At the centre of this work were the Motleys, who were his designers-in-chief. They had a studio in St Martin's Lane – once the workshop of Chippendale – and this became the central meeting place of the young actors, producers and designers revolving round Gielgud's semi-permanent company. There one found, besides Gielgud himself, Olivier, Redgrave, Byam Shaw, Guinness, Devine, Saint-Denis and many others whose work was beginning to flower. It was a place not only where the work was done, but where it could be talked about, and where many friendships and collaborations were formed. This also we owe the Motleys. Since that time this closely connected group has broken up, but I think the understanding between the members of it has remained.

This book is an example of yet another aspect of their work – their desire to communicate and teach what they have learned, not only as artists but as craftsmen, to the younger generation, professional or unprofessional, and for this task their complete knowledge of all the techniques of designing and making fits them well. I feel sure that this book can be of great practical use as well as being an illustrated record of work achieved.

Peggy Ashcroft

London, 1964

INTRODUCTION

'I met a fool in the forest, a Motley fool . . .
Motley's the only wear'

Jacques, *As You Like It*

For audiences in London, New York and around the world, over a period of more than forty years, the words 'Design by Motley' in the production credits of a play or film meant the very best in contemporary costume and set design. Beginning in 1932 with John Gielgud and his circle, Motley, consisting of Margaret Harris, her sister Sophie, and their friend Elizabeth Montgomery, soon dominated theatre design in the West End and at the Old Vic. In the 1940s they came to the fore on Broadway and at the Metropolitan Opera. Thereafter they expanded to the Royal Shakespeare Theatre, English National Opera, the avant-garde Royal Court and the American Shakespeare Festival. In all, until they retired in 1976, they designed costumes and sets for more than three hundred productions across the drama spectrum: Shakespeare, modern classics, new plays, opera, ballet, musicals and films. Their stage hits are a checklist of twentieth-century theatre greats – the Olivier–Gielgud *Romeo and Juliet*, Mary Martin's *South Pacific* and *Peter Pan*, *Il Trovatore* at the Metropolitan Opera, John Osborne's *Look Back in Anger*, Eugene O'Neill's *Long Day's Journey into Night* – to name only six from dozens. Of several films for which they designed costumes, *The Loneliness of the Long Distance Runner* and *The Spy Who Came in from the Cold* are perhaps the best known.

As interpreters of drama, the three Motley women were unusual among twentieth-century designers not only for the diversity and quantity of their work, but also for their dedication to the playwright, director and actors. In the best sense, theirs was the art that concealed art – not a flashy 'concept' stamped on the play, but costumes and set that helped the performers to give it shape and meaning. Since 1981 more than 5,000 of the designs have been preserved in the University of Illinois Library, thus extending Motley's vast theatrical legacy beyond the memories of the performers and playgoers. From them theatre historians can reconstruct Motley's work. In addition, this invaluable book, amply illustrated, offers the designers' own explanation of their methods and methodology.

Michael Mullin
Urbana, Illinois, 1991

1: THE WORK OF THE DESIGNER:
THE EVOLUTION OF A STAGE COSTUME

The creation of a stage costume begins necessarily with a reading of the play involved – an act which inevitably calls for some exercise of the designer's own critical faculties. Happily, however, so far as the designer is concerned, those faculties may usually be put to constructive use. Plays may be doomed by drama critics or put to death by unappreciative audiences, but they seldom expire upon the drawing-board. Few dramatic offerings are so poor that they cannot be helped by the designer's craft, few are so good that well-designed costumes are unnecessary. The fact that bad plays, as well as good, present a challenge to the costume artist is one of the more pleasant aspects of our profession. However, the challenge of either cannot be fairly met unless the designer has thoroughly familiarized himself with the play script and its characters.

THE SCRIPT Such familiarization can only result from a careful reading – and often re-reading many times – of the script. We ourselves make notes about the characters, setting down our own impressions of what each character, visually speaking, should finally become. We do so with the full knowledge that such preconceived notions may be rudely dealt with when we enter that preliminary production conference which is the next logical step in the evolution of a stage costume. The director's ideas can be, and often are, at wide variance with our own. But even the mightiest of directors will expect his collaborators to have opinions of their own. Silence may be golden in some fields, but in the theatre it can be mistaken for apathy or ignorance, and good is likely to come from discussions.

CONSULTING THE DIRECTOR The success of the designer depends in a large measure upon his collaboration with the director, who, in a very real sense, is like the highest ranking officer in a chain of command. For reasons of his own he may, so far as costumes are concerned, wish to emphasize certain characters, and to push others into the background; and he may place upon some or all characters a very different interpretation from your own. If he is a competent director he will make his ideas abundantly clear, and if he is a fair one he will weigh the merits of yours, and if he is a great director he will probably manage somehow to blend the best of your ideas with his own. If he is none of these things, there may be trouble ahead, although it has been our experience that most second-rate directors will usually let the designer's concepts prevail in the long run, yielding the field by a kind of default.

Out of the director-designer conference must come the decisions which determine the over-all, and the specific, manner in which the costume artist will approach the play. The director may want the actors dressed in clothes that are realistic copies of a period's fashions, or he may want them to wear imaginative versions which he believes will give a special meaning to the play and his interpretation of it, or he may seek to strike a balance between the real and the illusory. Designers are advised to reach an agreement as early as possible about the method of treatment preferred. After the decision is made – and only then – we draw rough preliminary sketches which mirror, as faithfully as possible, the director's ideas.

CONSULTING THE
DESIGNER

Once the important initial meeting with him has been held, an immediate conference with the set designer is usually scheduled. An ideal situation is one where the same designer is responsible for both costumes and settings. This is frequently the case in England, but many professional productions elsewhere – in New York especially – seem to favour a rather rigid separation of costumes and sets; it is almost as though the artists were invited to contend with each other in a kind of competition.

In such a case one meets the set designer and hopes for the best. The prudent costume designer ensures his hopes by choosing colours that harmonize with – and will not be overwhelmed by – the colours of the scenic background. Actually, since both artists are members of the same club, so to speak, co-operation can usually be counted on. Most costume and scenic designers realize that the efforts of one should complement those of the other, if the best interests of the production are to be served. The finest effects result when both artists work 'off the same palette'.

An understanding of the production's lighting plot is also essential if the costume designer hopes to get the best results, and conferences with whomever is responsible for stage illumination – director, set designer or lighting experts – are vitally necessary. The best of costumes can be 'drowned' in too much light, or lost in too little. There are, of course, colours and fabrics that have a fair chance of surviving even in a flood of light, and we will deal with them at another place. A scheme of colour can also be enhanced or damaged by the *colour* of the light.

VISUALIZING THE
ACTOR

Actors must be seen before they can be dressed, but many productions are not fully cast when the costume designer sets to work. Needless to say, one does not remain idle while waiting for all the roles to be filled. When we have submitted our first rough sketches to the director, and had them approved, we turn to colour, producing preliminary sketches which may also indicate, by appended bits of cloth, the kind of fabric which we wish to use – and the choice of fabrics is a vital part of the costume designer's work. If an actor seems securely assigned to a role, our colour sketches bear a reasonable resemblance to him. If not, they are more or less amorphous, awaiting a more finished sketch when the part has been filled.

Casting occasionally comes as a shock to the designer, rudely disrupting more or less firmly established conceptions of the characters, and sometimes giving rise to special problems which not only tax the designer's ingenuity ·but also demand consultations with experts in other fields.

For example, when we agreed to do the costumes for Maxwell Anderson's play, *Anne of the Thousand Days*, the leading male role had not been filled. Mr Anderson's hero was Britain's King Henry VIII, and in our preliminary sketches and planning we had quite naturally visualized him as the traditionally thick-set, burly monarch who had been portrayed on stage and screen by the late Charles Laughton and other actors running to rather more than ample girth and bulk. The final choice of Rex Harrison to play the part was a distinct surprise to us.

Mr Harrison eventually played Henry to critical acclaim, but before he could play him, he had reasonably to resemble him, and the slender Harrison was physically a far cry from a man who, as has been said, is known even in silhouette to half the literate world. Among other things, he had to have heavy and cumbersome legs, and such legs Rex Harrison definitely had not. A Hollywood 'expert' finally produced a pair to meet the requirements of our sketch, which was certainly a departure for us, if not for him. The royal underpinnings were made of rubber, moulded in monstrous guise.

Harrison must have felt, in them, like a strange being from outer space, but he wore them bravely, as he did the heavily padded costumes. The latter were designed in almost every respect to make him indeed appear burly, with a massive 'built-in' chest (padded with cotton wadding), and specially constructed high shoulders that had the visual effect of shortening the actor's neck. The set designer aided by designing narrow doorways which heightened the illusion of size and weight. The director, however, discarded most of the scenery during a Philadelphia tryout. Rex Harrison faced the opening-night audience against a small permanent set on a half empty stage, and the original Henry VIII himself might have appeared insignificant in such surroundings. Our only recourse was to increase the padding, and Harrison's performance was not only a dramatic *tour de force* but an exercise in physical endurance as well (see plate 22).

The production also called for somewhat unusual efforts in the field of research. It may be as well to touch upon these here, for research is a necessary part of the designer's work in nearly all productions, and few present more difficult problems than did *Anne*. The part of Henry VIII, as written, demanded many changes in costume. Audiences were expected to see him not only as Holbein and other artists saw him, but also in the Tudor equivalent of sporting dress, and in casual moments of undress such as few if any court painters ever recorded for posterity. We explored everything available in the way of contemporary painting, read all the material we could find concerning sixteenth-century dress, and were generally wary of those 'costume books' which illustrate a modern artist's own interpretation of the work of Tudor or Elizabethan painters. If, in *Anne*, we had to resort inevitably to some improvisation and let our imaginations off the leash, we did not permit them to run wild. Everything that Henry wore had some basis in historical fact.

SELECTING THE FABRIC

When the casting of a play has been finally completed, the costume designer goes to work in deadly earnest, and usually, unless the production is a slight one, on a 'fuller than full-time' schedule. We have indicated that the matter of fabrics is very important; now, with his colour sketches and his samples of fabric approved, the designer must procure the fabric itself.

It is, we believe, necessary to do one's own shopping; the designer who does not may find himself victimized not only by slip-shod assistants, but by sincere and conscientious ones as well, for the fabric plan is as much an integral part of the artist's scheme as his ideas of colour or line, and by its very nature a secret thing which cannot easily be communicated. Character in costume can be expressed by texture almost as well as by colour or design; the very manner in which a fabric drapes or folds can add to or detract from the finished product. It should be borne in mind that the effectiveness of a texture which will be seen in the 'large' can only be determined by the use of large samples; small patterns have a way of losing their veracity when exposed to bright lights and expanded dimensions. If it is not possible to examine your patterns under stage lights, you will be wise to view them under strong artificial illumination, and *never, never*, under fluorescent lamps, which distort colours completely.

We will deal with specific fabrics in a subsequent chapter, but no step-by-step discussion on stage costume evolution can be complete without a mention of fabric buying. It is one of our more important and arduous tasks, and one which is of course conditioned by the size of the production budget.

The designer may bask in the sun of a fat budget, or shiver in the shadow of a lean one, yet the obstacle presented by a small budget – or even a seemingly inadequate one – may often be surmounted. There is a wide variety of relatively inexpensive material suitable for use in costume making. One of the most successful Motley productions was John Gielgud's production of *Hamlet* (plates 1, 2), in which the costumes were made of scenery canvas, painted with dyes and metallic paints; bands of velveteen were the only trimmings used. In another Gielgud production, *The Merchant of Venice* (plate 4 and FIG. 1), we made the costumes of unbleached calico. Designs adapted from brocades in Italian paintings were drawn freehand on the calico, then painted with dyes.

It may be that luck as well as ingenuity guided us, but we were determined to avoid the use of tinsel, bright gilt braid, and other elaborate if inexpensive trappings which had bedecked costumes for many years. We were early convinced that such items are among the clichés of the craft, and we have always advised students against their use. In our opinion, there is almost no decorative effect that cannot be achieved without resorting to the hackneyed, and without resorting to a considerable outlay of money.

FIG 1
Designs for **The Merchant of Venice**

Once, during an enthusiastic, but financially ill-supported, production of *Macbeth* we employed wire brushes, purchased from an ironmonger, to simulate those huge silver ornaments which Scottish chiefs used to hold their plaids in place. Financial necessity was the mother of invention here, but we were anxious parents until the opening night curtain had been rung down. No one, however, complained about the ornaments, and to our relief they held the plaids secure.

CUTTING THE
COSTUME

A designer's work is far from completed with the submission of finished sketches and the purchase of fabrics; the execution of the costumes still remains, and it is perhaps the most arduous part of the entire assignment. The hard, mundane fact is that a competent designer must be, at least vicariously, a costume cutter, fitter and seamstress as well – and the less vicariously the better, since a designer *should* be able to turn out a finished garment, actually as well as theoretically. An elementary knowledge of cutting and sewing is certainly essential for the professional as well as the amateur – for constant help and supervision may be necessary in the work-room. Good cutters are, of course, artists themselves; but interpretation of a sketch is a very difficult and delicate process, and extraordinary things sometimes occur in the best of work-rooms, even when able practitioners are given detailed drawings and instructions.

Cutting is important to any garment, but in period costumes it can be all important. Relatively few persons professionally employed in making stage dress enjoy cutting period costumes as they were cut originally, and yet by the very manner in which seams are placed the authenticity of the costume may be achieved or lost. As students, we spent many hours in the National Gallery, and we went not to admire the techniques of painters, but to study the placing of seams. There are now several books available from which one may learn how almost all period costumes were made (see our recommended books); there are also museums in which vintage dresses are displayed, and many of these are most co-operative. When we were doing Katherine Hepburn's costumes for the film *Long Day's Journey Into Night*, the curator of a New York museum allowed Miss Hepburn to try on a priceless period dress. Pressed for time, we made an adaptation of the garment, in fabric and in style and, above all, in cut.

FITTING THE
COSTUME

In the professional theatre, after the cutting of the costume has been supervised and the garment has passed into the hands of those who sew it, the designer must attend at least two fittings as well as the final 'trying-on' which precedes the play's dress parade.

Amateur dress parades can be handled in much the same manner, for in both professional and amateur undertakings, every performer should, at some appointed time, put on his costume and walk under a light which as closely approximates that of the stage as possible. The costume should be looked at from every angle (front, back and side), and it is at this time that the actor should voice any complaints he may have. He should make sure he can sit, kneel, bow or do whatever he has to do in the costume.

It is a part of the professional designer's job – or at least it had better be – to see to it that the costumes are strongly made. Most stage clothes receive hard and constant wear, if the play be a success, and in his planning the designer must perforce regard a play's longevity as a foregone conclusion. This does not, of course, apply so much to amateurs as their productions are seldom put on for a long run.

Costumes worn in musicals, and other productions entailing energetic movement, pose a special problem. They must be strengthened at all points of strain and reinforced at the seams, but this must somehow be accomplished without distorting the garments' original lines.

If quick changes of costume are necessary, careful arrangements must be made for them; these may sometimes need to be elaborate, and on occasion stretch ingenuity to the breaking point. In *Anne of the Thousand Days*, both Rex Harrison and Joyce Redmond, his co-star, had a number of lightning-like changes, but some sort of record was probably set when both were required to change into full coronation dress in thirty seconds. Others among Harrison's heavy costumes had to be changed almost literally in a twinkling of an eye, and we had to invent a device by which they could, in effect, be 'snapped' on and off. Zippers had to be used for the coronation scene, but they were completely hidden. We strongly advise against the use of the ordinarily useful zippers in period costume, unless some means can be found of making the audience believe that authentic fastenings of the day have been employed. Velcro, of course, offers the costume designer another valuable method of fastening. It not only permits extremely quick fastening, but also has the advantage of being entirely invisible.

AGEING THE COSTUME

Many costumes need to be 'broken down' (artificially aged) and this, too, is a part of the designer's task. Costumes may be sprayed when it is possible, or if not, paint can be applied for this purpose with a sponge. The best tones for ageing, in our opinion, are black and khaki. The standard, quick-drying spray paints are available in metallic shades and many colours, but one can mix one's own shades for special purposes such as these, in a bottle or jar whose top may be adapted to an atomizer. Alternatively, dyes mixed with water or alcohol (as directed on their packets) can be sprayed on with an electric paint spray or, if the area is not too big, with a mouth spray such as artists use for fixing pastel drawings. Costumes can be bleached or even manhandled into a reasonable semblance of hard usage and antiquity, but great care should be taken to make wear apparent at places where wear would logically first occur – at basic seams, collars and cuffs, knees and trouser seats.

In *South Pacific* we bought many of the garments worn by the actors from a war surplus store, and literally beat, kicked and dragged them into a fine state of disrepair. In a 1961 production of *Troilus and Cressida* at the American Shakespeare Festival Theatre in Stratford, Connecticut, the director chose to costume the play in the period of the American Civil War. We were working on a low budget and, lacking means of making union or confederate uniforms, we obtained them from a New York *costumier*. A bale of almost obscenely new grey uniforms, complete with glittering brass buttons, had somehow to be made to resemble the tattered and faded rags worn by General Lee's starveling veterans in the last days of the great war. The back-stage carnage was awful; we ripped, clashed, sprayed and bleached with abandon, and we worked upon each costume, at places of natural strain, with wire brushes. If the results achieved were not entirely satisfactory, the exercise involved was certainly stimulating.

[1]

[2]

PLATES 1, 2   MOTLEY

Ophelia (Jessica Tandy) and a lady of the
court in **Hamlet,** directed by John Gielgud in
1934. These costumes were made of scenery
muslin, sprayed with analine dye. Velveteen
was the only trimming. The chain necklaces
were crocheted in rubber cord and sprayed
with metallic paint. The designs on the
costumes were stencilled in gold, silver,
and copper.

[3]

[4]

[5]

[6]

PLATE 5   MOTLEY

A squire in **Richard II**, directed by John Gielgud
in 1937. The squire's tabard was made of felt and
the heavy leather belt was decorated with a row
of studs.

PLATE 6   MOTLEY

The Queen (Peggy Ashcroft) in **Richard II**, directed
by John Gielgud in 1937. This costume was olive
green moire, stencilled with silver leaves.

[8]

PLATE 7 LILA DE NOBILI

Sir Andrew (Richard Johnson) in **Twelfth Night**, directed by Peter Hall in 1958.

PLATE 8 ANTHONY POWELL

Bianca (Jeanne Hepple) in **Women Beware Women**, directed by Anthony Page in 1962.

[10]

[9]

[11]

[12]

PLATE 9 ROGER FURSE

Juliet (Claire Bloom) in **Romeo and Juliet,** directed
by Hugh Hunt in 1952.

PLATE 10 MOTLEY

Juliet (Dorothy Tutin) in **Romeo and Juliet,** directed
by Glen Byam Shaw in 1958.

PLATE 11 MOTLEY

Juliet (Zena Walker) in **Romeo and Juliet,** directed
by Glen Byam Shaw in 1954.

PLATE 12 MOTLEY

Juliet (Peggy Ashcroft) in **Romeo and Juliet,**
directed by John Gielgud in 1935.

[13]

[14]

[15]

[16]

PLATE 13   MOTLEY

Nurse (Rosalind Atkinson) in **Romeo and Juliet,** directed by Glen Byam Shaw in 1954.

PLATE 14   MOTLEY

Nurse (Edith Evans) in **Romeo and Juliet,** directed by John Gielgud in 1935.

PLATE 15   MOTLEY

Romeo (Laurence Harvey) in **Romeo and Juliet,** directed by Glen Byam Shaw in 1954.

PLATE 16   MOTLEY

Tybalt (Geoffrey Toone) in **Romeo and Juliet,** directed by John Gielgud in 1935.

[17]

[18]

PLATE 17   LESLIE HURRY

Diomedes (David Buck) in **Troilus and Cressida**, directed by Peter Hall in 1960.

PLATE 18   TANYA MOISEIWITSCH

Oedipus (James Mason) in **Oedipus Rex**, directed by Tyrone Guthrie in 1958.

[19]

25

[20]

[21]

PLATE 20　MOTLEY

Becket (Laurence Olivier), directed by Peter Glenville, in 1960. Becket's cape was stencilled linen, gold on black.

PLATE 21　MOTLEY

Queen (Margaret Hall) in **Becket**, directed by Peter Glenville in 1960. This dress, of apple green raw silk with gold cord appliqué, called for lilac pink in the under sleeves and sleeve linings.

PLATE 22　MOTLEY

Henry VIII (Rex Harrison) in **Anne of the Thousand Days,** directed by H. C. Potter in 1948. In order to make Rex Harrison resemble King Henry VIII, a good deal of padding was built into the chest and shoulders. The basic costume consisted of wallflower brown velvet over wool tunic, gold braid appliqué, sleeves studded with gold. The necklace was made of antique gold cloth on stiff canvas, decorated with sized felt Tudor roses and pearls. He wore a black velvet hat with a cream ostrich feather.

[22]

PLATE 23   MOTLEY

Desdemona (Margaret Johnston) in **Othello,** directed by Glen Byam Shaw in 1956.

PLATE 24   MOTLEY

Becket (Laurence Olivier), directed by Peter Glenville, in 1960. The horse's canopy was made of felt, appliqued in felt and braid.

PLATE 25   PETER HALL

Romeo (John Stride) in **Romeo and Juliet,** directed by Franco Zefferelli in 1961.

[23]

[24]

[26]

MOTLEY

PLATE 26   MOTLEY

Grouped characters in **Il Trovatore**, directed
by Dr. Herbert Graf in 1959. The nun's
head-dress was made of white buckram,
pleated, and the robe of black wool. The other
gowns were made of raw silk.

PLATE 27   MOTLEY

Azucena (Giulietta Simionato) in **Il Trovatore**,
directed by Dr. Herbert Graf in 1959. The
wool in this costume was sprayed and aged
to give a faded appearance.

[27]

[28]

[29]

PLATES 28, 29 PETER RICE

Dancing Master (Alexander Young) and a lady
of the chorus in **Ariadne,** directed by Anthony
Besch in 1961.

There are many ways of tackling the business of breaking down a costume. Knees and elbows can be rubbed with pumicestone or a wire brush, and treated with soap or candle wax at places where shine would occur. The garment itself can be damped and the pockets filled with heavy weights. If it needs to look wet on the stage, the only satisfactory thing to do is to damn the consequences and use real water; such substitutes as glycerine or oil are only partly successful. Burning is the best way of making wear holes and frayed edges, boot polish brushed on hard is another good 'ager', and Fuller's earth, which can be bought at any chemist's store, will give a good effect of dust when sprinkled on. In general, the darker shades of pancake make-up are excellent for breaking down, and have the great advantage of being easily removable by dry cleaning.

DESIGNING THE ACCESSORIES

The designer's responsibility is not ended when the costume, as such, has been completed, for *everything* worn by the actor should be made or bought under the costume artist's supervision. Hats, wigs, gloves, shoes, all the accessories that 'finish off' stage dress are a part of the finished design; so are hand 'props' such as purses and parasols and walking-sticks; so, in some cases, are articles of underclothing. Research is usually necessary in this last field, and problems of real magnitude occasionally arise. For example in *The Majority of One*, Cedric Hardwicke, playing an affluent Japanese businessman, had to display the kind of unmentionables worn by respectable Japanese gentlemen of the present day. We found no such underwear depicted in costume books or available in Manhattan's Japanese shops, although kimonos and other garments needed could readily be had in Fifth Avenue establishments. Sir Cedric's lingerie was finally imported from Tokyo, leaving us to wonder just what sort of under-garments might be worn by wealthy Japanese in New York.

The designer should also speak with authority so far as make-up and coiffure are concerned; bad make-up or hair style can ruin even the most effective costume. In Hollywood, there exists what some harried designers must almost believe to be a sinister conspiracy against the tasteful and the authentic in hair-styling. Stage hairdressers in London and New York are usually more amenable to the demands of the designer, directors more sensitive to the requirements of the script, actresses less determined to play 'Lady Teazle' with a present-day hair-do. Yet even in these capitals of the theatrical world, one must often fight to get what one wants.

It is a fight worth waging, for the appearance of the head is of vital importance to the designer, and upon it may well depend the success or failure of any costume. If hair styles and wigs, hats and head-dresses are visually right, even the most simple and economical costumes may carry conviction. Conversely, if they are palpably wrong, then the most beautiful and authentic of garments may find their effectiveness impaired or utterly destroyed: a cheap permanent wave can completely undo an expensive, carefully built illusion.

APPROVING THE FINAL PRODUCT

With costumes finished and all accessories in hand, the designer arranges a first dress parade – which should take place at least a week before the dress rehearsal, to allow time for alteration. There, for the first time, the director sees your work complete almost in every detail; there also he decides whether or not your visual interpretations match his own. Notes are made which indicate necessary changes, and with

FIG 2
Small rough sketches for **Othello**

great luck, all aspects of fit and appearance may be finally approved. The designer now awaits, and usually with some pardonable anxiety, the dress rehearsal (in the professional theatre, the first of several). The dress rehearsal is, in a large sense, the costume artist's 'moment of truth', for now the clothes are put to practical use and ultimate test – moved in, walked in, breathed in, acted in, their worth either proved or disproved by the animation which at best a designer can have only imagined. Whatever changes follow are largely anti-climactic, and so may be even the opening night performance, for by then the artist has passed his point of no return.

These, then, are the tasks of the costume designer, the work performed progressively in carrying one's ideas forward from drawing-board to curtain rise. Some of them are burdensome, some pleasant almost to the point of personal exaltation; but none of them may be shirked. Designing is an exacting profession. We do not recommend it for the faint-hearted or the indolent, and we presume that those who read the following pages will be neither. In them we will explain in detail the methods and techniques that we have found advantageous, although the success of the aspirant designer must ultimately depend upon his own ingenuity, and his capacity for hard work, originality and talent. We believe that the effort can be in some ways even more rewarding than the work of the creative painter. After all, even Botticelli never saw the beautiful clothes he painted come alive, worn by the finest performing talents of the age.

2: THE COSTUME SKETCH: METHODS AND MATERIALS

A forgotten American humourist once said that all men – including doctors – should have at least an elementary knowledge of anatomy. For obvious reasons, that generalization embraces stage designers, too; and even in an age in which many artists *feel* more than they draw or paint, the designer must have some understanding of draftsmanship. One need not be a Da Vinci to create an effective costume sketch, but some amount of technical skill is certainly necessary, at least enough to make your drawing intelligible to those who must work with it. That skill can usually be acquired. All men cannot be taught to draw, any more than all dogs can be taught to walk upon their hind legs – but few dogs probably have any earnest desire to walk otherwise than upon all fours. Of men who sincerely wish to learn to draw, most men can.

THE FIRST SKETCH We ourselves worked at portraiture, and at commercial illustrating, before entering the designing field, and attended art schools before we ever did any of those things. Study of the human figure was, of course, compulsory, and we have made use of it, although our preliminary sketches for a production might leave that assertion open to some doubt. But these are, as we have said, merely a means of conveying our ideas to the director, who realizes they are no more a finished product than his own work is, at that early stage. We have found that a good method is to rough out small figures in costume on cartridge paper or on sheets from a pad of cheap drawing paper available in any artists' material shop. These can then be spread out and seen in groups, as they will appear in the various scenes of the play, and the balance of shape, character and colour can be more easily judged than they would be with larger sketches (see Figs. 1, 2).

PAPER Sketches that pass out of the designer's hands should be produced upon durable material, paper tough enough to withstand the rough handling the drawings are almost certain to receive. A young designer of our acquaintance turned a sheaf of exquisite sketches, done upon expensive but flimsy paper, over to a director who returned them, tattered and almost obliterated, after they had been examined by only his production staff and himself. On the other hand, the durability factor can also be over-emphasized. We once did the sketches for a musical on rather heavy cardboard, and as the production wore on and more and more costumes were added, finally found ourselves literally unable to carry them all about.

Most designers prefer strong water colour paper obtainable in almost any developed part of the world, and even in some areas not noted for the amenities: on a remote Caribbean island, we found a very good grade of paper, although our requests for 'poster paints' were greeted by blank stares. We use an absorbent, rough-textured paper which can be obtained in blocks of varying quantities and sizes, and with extremely heavy cardboard backs which in themselves act as a sort of drawing-board. If a thinner paper is used the designs should be mounted on thin cardboard.

PAINTS Most designers work with inexpensive poster colours, which come in jars (Rich Art), the more costly designers' gouache, which comes in tubes (Winsor and Newton), or acrylics. The designers' colours are made in a larger range. Designers can apply the thick, quick-drying paints over pencilled outlines, or instead use a grey crayon, the colour of which is lost when the paint is brushed on, or even simply put the paint on to the paper with no outline at all.

BRUSHES Most art supply stores have a stock of cheap brushes on hand, the prices of the better varieties being what they are; but the cheaper ones simply won't stand much use, and have a way of disintegrating at most inconvenient times. In the long run, the very best kind of sable brushes will prove an economy, although the cost of them may make one wonder if the sable has not become one of the rarest beasts on earth.

PREPARING THE
SKETCH Water colours should not be washed on thinly, but applied as 'solidly' as possible. In most professional productions, various work-room managers estimate competitively on the making of the costumes, and your sketches may pass through many hands while estimates are being made. Samples of the fabrics you wish to use should be affixed securely to the sketches with glue or by stapler.

Instructions to work-rooms are often pencilled on the margins of the drawings, which are sometimes protected by plastic covers; if they are not, it will be as well to print the instructions boldly, in ink (see FIG. 3). If your production is a large and involved one, and there are many costumes, it is advisable to have photostats made; since you merely want a record of what you have done, a considerable number of drawings can be reproduced upon a single photostat sheet. They will be in black-and-white, of course, but if some of your colour sketches should be mislaid in the work-room, they at least help you to remember what pigments were used in the missing sketches. Colour Xerox provide a useful, if expensive alternative.

Each costume in a play, from those worn by the stars down to that of the lowliest 'super', will usually require an individual drawing. Occasionally, in depicting mass movement, we sketch a group of figures upon a wide sheet of paper (FIG. 4); and in Shakespearean productions, we draw soldiery in wide-spread marching columns, in an attempt to create for ourselves – and the director – some of the sweep and spirit and vigour of a military advance. Each character, however, is reproduced singly before we turn our sketches over to the work-room, and we aim at avoiding the 'stereotype' by making each sketch subtly different, giving some personal touch even to uniforms and armour, if only a slight variation in colour values. In musicals and ballets, chorus personnel who wear identical costumes can be drawn *en masse*, but the work of execution will be easier if individual sketches are made.

The actor should be given the chance of seeing the costume designs as early as possible; they may have an effect on the way he thinks of the part, or he may have very

BARTHOLOMEW FAIR

QUARLOS
ESMOND KNIGHT

BLACK FELT HAT.
BLACK AND WHITE UNCURLED
OSTRICH FEATHERS.
PEARL EARRINGS.

WHITE ORGANDY COLLAR AND
CUFFS. WITH WHITE MACRAMÉ
LACE EDGING. WHITE
LAWN UNDER SLEEVES.

STIFF CRIMSON SATIN
SUIT. THE WAIST
CUT MUCH HIGHER
THAN NATURAL
WAIST-LINE
MELON SHAPED
BREECHES ON
STIFF INTERLINING.
BLACK VELVET POINTS
(WITH SILVER TAGS)
AND GARTERS (WITH
SILVER FRINGE)

CRIMSON WOOL. OR
DULL NYLON TIGHTS.
BLACK SUEDE BOOTS
WITH SPURS AND
SPUR GUARDS.
BLACK SUEDE GLOVES
TRIMMED WITH SILVER.
BLACK SUEDE SWORD
BELT.

CLOAK. (CIRCULAR)
BLACK. SMOOTH CLOTH.
HEAVY ENOUGH TO BE
UNLINED. EDGE
CUT. WITH NO HEM

BLUE MOIRÉ OR TAFFETA
SASH.

MOTLEY '50

FIG 3
Workroom instructions on a sketch
for **Bartholomew Fair**

FIG 4
Group of sailors in **Henry V**

strong feelings that the costume will not help him to get the character he wants. His feelings and ideas should be most carefully considered and discussed with the director and himself and incorporated in the design whenever possible.

We usually lay out a little exhibition of the costume designs at the first rehearsal or reading of the play, pinning or taping the sketches to the walls of the rehearsal room, to screens or to the backs of flats. This allows all the actors to see not only what their own costume will be like, but also how all the people they are playing with will look.

THE STUDIO   Every artist probably dreams of a clean, airy studio with a good north light, and one that preferably never fails, but for many designers, especially beginners, such ideal accommodations may be impossible to obtain. (And for amateurs, of course, the possibility of a studio at all seldom arises.) We have worked in some strange and widely varied places: on a cranky small table in an hotel room in Stratford-upon-Avon, a garden bench in Trinidad, the concrete lip of the pool in Wembley Stadium, a 'private' bungalow-studio on the Selznick lot in Hollywood, and once, in dire extremity, at the top of a flight of stairs. Although art thrives in garrets not because of garrets, but in spite of them, surroundings are not *all* that important. The dedicated designer ought to be able to work, if necessary, in Grand Central Station – and may have to.

The tools of the costume designer are relatively few, the techniques – up to a point – relatively simple. Methods of work vary, of course, with the individual craftsman, but we will wager that all methods have one common denominator: the need to expedite the work on hand. Stage designers, almost alone among artists, must work with production dates firmly fixed and usually rigidly adhered to. For the designer working against a relentless 'dead-line', time is a bird with a rapid wing.

3: YOUR PALETTE: THE USES
OF COLOUR IN COSTUME DESIGN

'My choice of colours does not rest on any scientific theory; it is based on observation, on feeling, on the very nature of such experience.' *Henri Matisse*

The artist-wit, James Whistler, said that mauve was merely pink trying to be purple. The statement revealed not only some of his own demonstrably great knowledge of colour, but also a reasonable amount of prejudice; Mr Whistler quite obviously did not care for mauve. The prejudice is understandable; even most laymen, as well as artists, dislike certain colours, just as they like others. We have said that most men can learn to draw, and although truly great colourists are probably born, not made, we are convinced that the dedicated artist can develop an effective colour sense. The opinions expressed here are the result of years of experience – and experiment – combined with personal preferences. Colour is an intimate and individual thing, and cannot be subjected to any arbitrary rules – except one's own.

USING COMPATIBLE COLOURS

Experience has convinced us that one of our theories is absolutely sound: colour values, their depths, their intensities, rather than pigments themselves, are the cause of effective colour schemes. For example, colours that we normally think of as being unpleasant together, may be blended harmoniously if they are far enough apart in value. Certain shades of green and purple or brown and blue may be too close in value, but by using a dark green with pale lilac, a deep purple with pale green, or dark brown with pale blue, you can achieve beautiful results.

Blue and yellow together are anathema to us personally. But even if it were absolutely necessary to use them, they could be rendered attractive by choosing a pale grey-blue and a deep greenish-yellow or an indigo blue and a pale greyed-yellow.

On the other hand, various shades of one colour can be almost always successfully blended; under stage lighting almost all reds, oranges and other shades in the red 'family', look well together (see plate 47). Pink stage light somehow manages to make all these colours go grey and is fatal to them, as indeed it is to all colours; despite some directors' reliance upon it, the fact is that pink light 'muddies' pigments. Pale amber or straw light, on the other hand, has a salutary effect upon reds; it brings out their warmth and positively makes them glow. Steel blue and white are the best of all possible choices for bringing out the illumination of colour.

RESTRICTING YOUR PALETTE

Limiting your palette to a few colours is usually better than trying to employ an enormous variety. The principal characters in any production must stand out: reds, whites and blacks are colours that will make them do so. This is an over-simplification,

39

of course, but as a general rule, the costumes of the principals should be either the darkest or the lightest or the most brilliant of your designs.

When designing clothes for early periods, we advise using colours as close as possible to those which were achieved by using primitive vegetable dyes; modern chemical dye colours should be scrupulously avoided if possible. Available Oriental fabrics of the present period, such as raw silk, are valuable to the designer because these give the appearance of being rough woven material, as were the fabrics produced by hand workmanship in earlier times. On stage, a textured material is always more rich looking than one with a completely smooth surface, for colours have more depth and gain in intensity. As we have stated, over-dyeing will result in a rich, textured look. Black-and-white tweeds are particularly suitable for this purpose.

OBTAINING
THE COLOUR
YOU WANT

Compromise is as necessary in the world of the theatre as it is in statesmanship, although seldom achieved by such subtle and genteel means; but we are opposed to it in the matter of colour. Dye fabrics exactly the colour you want, rather than approximately that colour. We have spoken harshly of modern chemical dyes for period pieces, but since the designer lacks the means of making vegetable dyes, the designer must work with those at hand. Some of the ill effects of chemical dyes can be offset by judicious mixing. Professional dyeing establishments can usually be prevailed upon to match your colour sample exactly, or at least nearly so. For amateur productions, stage wear may be dyed by the designers themselves. For professional costumes, frequent dry cleaning will be required and the colours must be fast; hence you should go to an expert in the dyeing field. Most of the big subsidised companies now run their own dyeing and fabric painting departments and can achieve excellent results.

In musical productions the costumes are extremely important for setting moods – far more so perhaps than in straight dramatic plays. Musical plots are usually slight in nature and certainly afford greater scope for the designer's talents. Ballets are almost always included in such productions, and these may require exceptionally fantastic costumes. The over-all spectacle of mass choruses adds impact to the performance. In choruses for some operas, however, we believe that these subordinate characters should be seen largely as a background and a complement to the leading artistes. The effect should be as a wash of scenic colour rather than as individual costume portraits, many singers thus being treated as a unit.

In costume design for film or television there are special problems. You need to learn how colours will look embalmed in celluloid or video tape. The kind of film used will affect the colour. With certain kinds of film, for example, something like faded denim will appear a very shiny blue. The use of white varies according to the preferences of the cinematographer; some prefer whites to be considerably dulled. With television all colours and tones are exaggerated so that primary colours tend to scream and sometimes vibrate. Blacks and whites are very much affected, so 'TV grey', a surprisingly dark shade, is used for white. Certain colours 'bleed' on television, that is, the tone is dissipated by the light and outlines appear frayed. Blue is a culprit. Although scarlet bleeds badly, shocking pink will stay sharp. Some patterned fabrics can give poor images. For both film and television it is essential to consult the cinematographer on lighting and to get approval for all colours, as their preferences and attitudes vary enormously.

Colour is one of the chief methods of creating mood and giving a feeling of the locale, and even climatic conditions can be indicated by the use of pigment. Against a torrid Mexican setting, we used earth tones – 'hot' oranges and yellows – to achieve the feeling of aridity, and in some costumes have worked in violets and blue-greys to effect a sort of penumbra between the hot simulated sun of the stage lights and the deep shadows of the background. These colours were not only extremely effective visually but also reflected the authentic hues of the Mexican locality. A widely different palette can also create mood. In a production of *Macbeth* we sought to depict the intensity of the characters and the brooding Scottish landscape itself by using blacks, deep purples, the dark red of dried blood, indigoes and splotches of livid green and white. These tonal effects heightened the drama and conveyed the feeling of primitive times and strong emotions.

We have found it very useful to save a cutting of every piece of fabric we use and all the discarded patterns left over from shopping expeditions. If these are divided into colours and kept in separate boxes or in the drawers of a small cabinet – one for red, one for blue, etc. – they form an invaluable library of colour and texture.

The patterns on plate 47 illustrate some examples of colour combinations which compare those too near in value with colours that are in contrast and therefore more pleasing.

4: INTERPRETING CHARACTER THROUGH DESIGN

Stage costume can express many things. By its colour, it can show mood and taste; by its texture, economic status; by its style, both occupation and nationality. It is from a happy union of these qualities that character and credibility are born.

In developing character progressively throughout a play, the clothes of the actor may be of enormous value to his performance. For example, in Shakespeare's *Richard II*, the king appears in the beginning of the play as a frivolous young popinjay and ends his role as a betrayed and tragic prisoner. Here costumes must be made, by adroit use of colour, line, weight and style, to show clearly the sequence of events, and developments in the character of the luckless king.

All costume sketches, to be truly effective, should show character as clearly as possible, in style, in colour, and even in make-up. The smallest details can be helpful. The proportions, the pigment and texture of the fabric, the cut, the way it fits (well or badly), the most minute parts of decorations and accessories – all are important.

PROPORTION

In the designing and making of a stage costume that interprets character, a knowledge of proportion is essential – if only because he who understands it can better distort it. By proportion we mean the proportion and shape of the body in relation to the costume. This can be altered by padding and fit, and by such things as fullness and length of skirt, position of waistline, width of shoulders, length of sleeve, balance of colour and tone values, the size of the design or pattern on the fabric.

There are occasions in which proportion, seen in mass, results in a uniformity that inevitably detracts from the effectiveness of individual characterizations. The task of subtly distorting uniformity, without destroying the desired illusion, is a difficult one but a rewarding one from the designer's standpoint. Anton Chekhov's play, *The Three Sisters*, presents a case in point. The characters of the male players are clearly defined in Chekhov's writing, but because the men are all wearing military uniforms they are theoretically as similar in appearance as any designer of army apparel could ever wish

FIG 5
Uniform for different characters

a Smart and very military:
high collar, and buttons sloped
towards waist; right length
for sleeves and trousers

b Low collar, buttons much more
parallel, sleeves and trousers
a little too short

his subjects to be. One of the few ways in which the stage designer can help to differentiate between characters is by the alteration of proportion in relation to the wearer. It is a practice that military martinets would scarcely approve of, but stage designers fortunately serve in another area of authority.

To solve this problem, it is necessary to resort to small details, or, rather, to subtle distortions of such. A half-inch added to the size of a collar may make a figure seem less of a military stereotype and more of an ordinary man. Sleeves either a little too long or too short, or a coat too tightly fitting, can permit a martial tunic to take on something of the real character of its wearer (FIG. 5).

Alterations such as these, which do not show enough from the 'front' to make the uniforms seem strange to the audience, can be extremely effective, as well as helpful to the actor. In a London production of *The Three Sisters*, Sir Michael Redgrave wore a coat with a collar that was too low; Sir John Gielgud one that was too high. No one in the audience was unaware of the characters' individuality, the talents of these actors being what they are, but the small details added to the scope of their performances.

ACCESSORIES

The size and shape of patterns on the fabric have considerable importance in creating character; so have all details of trimming and decoration. Accessories should be absolutely in keeping with the costume. Jewellery, to be entirely effective, must be made to 'carry' on the stage. Decorative and inventive jewellery, made from braids, pearls, beads, pieces of coloured glass, etc., is more successful than the genuine article whose small details are lost upon the audience.

Shoes, which may be elegant or shabby, low or high-heeled, simple or elaborate, can be a valuable indication of the wearer's stage character. Few articles of apparel are more closely identified with a period than the foot-wear of a particular time, and substitutions can easily be recognized for the anachronisms that they are. And, needless to say, the style and fit of a shoe affects the manner in which a performer walks, and inferior or uncomfortable foot-wear may detract from a performance.

Head-dresses, hats, hair styles and wigs are all important in the delineation of authentic period and character, and often afford the designer an opportunity to bring out the individualism which a playscript demands. But unless meticulous attention is given to the matters of head-coverings and hair styles, no costume, however exquisite, can be complete, nor will the performer be all that the playwright desired him. Very careful drawings and colours sketches should be made for the wigmaker and hair stylist, and some actors like to have a sketch for their make-up. Such a sketch should certainly be provided if any special style is wanted.

CHOOSING THE
CORRECT FABRIC

Expression of character in stage costumes can also be aided by wise choice in fabric and texture. The hard brilliance of satin, the richness of velvet and silk, are obviously for people of elegance and wealth. Conversely, the cheaper fabrics – hessian, cotton, calico, linen and rough woollens – are more appropriate for the simple costumes of rural characters and persons in less affluent circumstances. Some stylized productions have been successful in which one of the more simple materials was used throughout. Notable in this category was John Gielgud's *Hamlet* (plates 1, 2), in which all the costumes were made of scenery canvas, painted with dyes and metallic pigments in gold, silver and copper sometimes sprayed on round a masked out design. The trimming used was velveteen, which contrasted well with the flat canvas. Gielgud's *Hamlet*, however, was a departure from decorative orthodoxy, in which the artists had an opportunity to create character through the use of unusual materials. Such field days for the stage designer are rare.

Linking the past to the present is a device that has been found to be helpful to the designer in building character. For example (and this may be an over-simplification of the idea) Brittanicus in Shaw's *Caesar and Cleopatra*, is readily identifiable as a certain type of Englishman. The first director and designer who equipped Brittanicus with a handle-bar moustache may have been gilding the lily, so to speak, but they did expedite the play's meaning by making him more easily recognizable as a comic foil to the more volatile Latins. We like to advise students to experiment with drawings in which they take classic figures of the drama and try to identify them with celebrated personalities of our own time – or for that matter, with any contemporary person. In one particular production of *Twelfth Night*, where the producer called for a more subtle interpretation of the character Sir Toby Belch, we chose to *think* of him as a country squire whose bucolic personality was evident through slightly more distinctive and less dreary country dress.

USING MODERN DRESS

Most period plays will offer an opportunity for such expansion. So, too, will most modern-dress productions of classics, although in them the designer is almost as much at the mercy of the director as is the audience; designers may be as bemused as the spectators at productions of *Hamlet* in which actors firmly clutching Victorian umbrellas speak of 'ungartered hose', or productions of *Troilus and Cressida* in which the hero wears the uniform of an American Civil War general.

Some modern dress ventures, however, have been happier; one offers a classic although simple idea of how character can be 'set', virtually at the rise of a curtain. In a modern dress version of *Julius Caesar*, Caesar and Antony wore the smart uniforms of Italian fascists. The director may have been belabouring the obvious by so doing, but Brutus wore casual mufti – a loose jacket and a flowing tie – which made him at first sight the direct antithesis of all that Caesar and his followers stood for.

Creating character through costume is, as we have said, difficult but it is a necessary skill and one that may certainly be improved through practice. Plays in which actors portray stereotypes are seldom successful; almost every character, as written, has some idosyncrasy which a designer may discover and develop, in collaboration with the director and actor – if he will try hard enough to find it.

FIG 6
Design for costume in **Hamlet**. The pattern was cut out in strong brown paper and pinned flat to the surface of the canvas, which was then sprayed with dye. When dry, the paper was removed, leaving its shape in undyed canvas, with the edges attractively blurred. This shape was then painted with metallic or coloured paint.

5: THE MEANING OF STAGE AND COSTUME PROPERTIES

A property, by accepted popular definition, is any article which is not a complete costume or scenic background, and, in a broad sense, any part of theatrical decor which is transportable within the confines of the setting itself. A property such as Lady Teazle's fan is an ingredient of a finished production, as important in its own way as is the great lumbering wagon that looms like another character in Brecht's *Mother Courage*; the stake at which Joan of Arc dies is a property, and so is the chain that binds her, and from the daggers of *Julius Caesar* to the trick drinking glass in *The Complaisant Lover*, all properties are a vital part of a play's development. The designer who creates them – especially the smaller articles – must often work with materials of which he knows little, adapting himself to techniques of which he knows less, to evoke 'finished' products that may bear no ultimate resemblance to the basic materials at all. And his ingenuity may be taxed as it is in no other field of endeavour.

COSTUME AND SCENIC DESIGNERS

Under ordinary circumstances, the costume designer is given the responsibility of creating, adapting or purchasing only those articles which are accessories to costume. These are called costume properties – as opposed to stage properties, which are more closely related to the scenery. Yet there are no absolutes in the matter of determining the procurement of properties, and jurisdiction is often mixed – and clouded – between the scenic and costume designer. Most resident companies employ specialists in property making, but such workers seldom if ever design the properties they build. There is a sort of twilight zone of operations between the tasks of the scenic and costume designer, into which each may occasionally wander; if there is any disagreement the director must be the final arbiter and authority.

To be specific, by the dictates of custom, swords and daggers and bandoliers are costume properties, but banners and heraldic devices are not; these should be part of the scene designer's province. The costume designer is expected to provide nosegays or bouquets carried by hand, but baskets of flowers and other larger floral pieces are the scene designer's responsibility, *unless* the director otherwise decrees. We italicize because the director often does decree, in the knowledge that a costume designer's colour scheme can be confused by that of the details which intimately surround it. In a profession in which, at first glance, we found our property contribution limited to such items as walking sticks and parasols, fans, purses, jewellery, eye-glasses, professional equipment and manually borne weapons, etc., we have been called upon to create imitation animals, out-sized heraldic devices and enormous banners, specially wrapped gift packages, exotic flowers such as no botanist could ever identify, and,

on one memorable occasion, oddments of space-age furniture disgorged from a disintegrating stage aeroplane.

**DIRECTOR
AND COSTUME
DESIGNER**

All adequate property plans – known as 'plots' in the idiom of the profession –
begin in conference with the director; all good ones evolve through constant con-
sultation. The competent director realizes that every 'prop' must have a meaning –
and that *none*, however important, must be permitted to present a visual distraction
that may impair the effectiveness of any actor's performance. A wise director knows
at what point Quasimodo's hump becomes grotesque rather than pathetic, or at what
length Cyrano's nose becomes not tragic, but absurd. A designer is indeed fortunate
if he works with a director who owns such powers of discrimination. He is even more
fortunate if his director understands the hard, fundamental rules of practical property
making, as they affect the budget, the finished production, and the artist himself. The
best way to avoid avoidable mistakes is for the designer to attend rehearsals whenever
possible, so that he may see for himself how each prop is to be used.

**DESIGNING
THE PROP**

A practical property is, as its name implies, a thing to be used, and (it is confidently
expected by all concerned from designers to optimistic financial backers of the production) subjected to long and constant wear. Designers who have to contend with
taut production deadlines sometimes leave property lists to be coped with at the last
moment – and usually do so to their sorrow. If possible, an early production meeting
should be fixed, at which all details of the property plot should be carefully considered.
There must be a complete list of all articles that will be required – subject, of course,
to last minute changes. Whether or not the production has two budgets – some have
one for costume, one for scenery – the bills must be paid, and it is an unwise designer
who is not aware, to the penny, of the maximum amount that may be spent. And if
there *is* one budget for costumes and another for scenery, the designer is advised to
acquire awareness of the maximums.

It is almost invariably necessary to make a sketch of each prop, and scale drawings
are usually required for intricate or large pieces. If you employ assistants or sub-
contractors to execute your designs, it will be well for you to do your own research, or,
failing that, give this chore only to trusted associates, and never permit execution

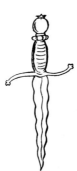

FIG 7
Sword and daggers

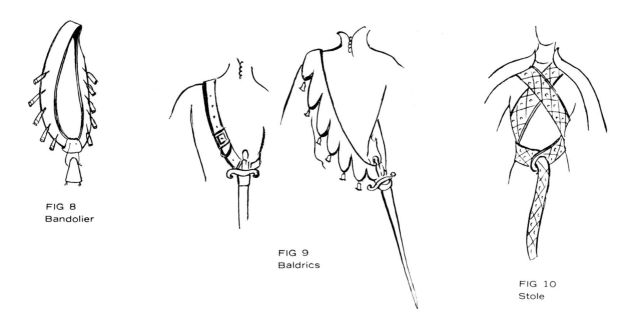

FIG 8
Bandolier

FIG 9
Baldrics

FIG 10
Stole

until you are satisfied that those who do the work have a complete understanding of what you want. Above all, colour patterns or paint samples should be provided. And, unless you are very familiar with the workmanship of those who will make your props, we advise you not to discuss matters of proportion or colour over the telephone, or to allow too much creative 'leeway' in the execution of your designs.

A time schedule for properties should be made – and made to coincide with the costume work-room schedules. Props that must 'work' on stage should be checked and re-checked to ensure strength and movability. Properties which actors use should be provided well before production date, so that they can get used to the shape and size and know how to handle them. Military orders, medals and chains and other articles that are to be put on or removed as part of stage business – these items must be made to fasten securely with strong clasps or pins, and to work easily, and they should never present a problem to the performer. Finally, in case the director demands last minute changes, there should be some provisions for the time and personnel necessary to complete the job.

MAKING THE PROP   Let us suppose that *you* are about to become a competitor in the field of stage property making. What, you may ask, will you be expected to make? The blunt, unequivocal answer is: anything!

Bear in mind at the outset that there are no hard and fast rules governing the making of stage properties, and that human ingenuity is the largest factor involved. However, it may be said that stage properties fall roughly into three categories: things that must seem, in an illusory sense, to be 'larger than life', things that are actually lighter than life, and things that are cheaper than life.

The first refers to items so small that their details are 'lost' in the distances that separate actors and audiences, and must be made, by various processes of exaggeration, to seem closer to the beholder than they are in reality. The second applies to heavy swords, shields, armorial accessories and other weighty weaponry – in short, to all articles, including crowns, mitres and heavy head-dresses, in which weight is a factor: the brawniest of present-day actors might find it difficult to give a convincing, mobile performance of *Richard III* if freighted with all the genuine accoutrements that monarch wore at Bosworth Field. In the third, the 'cheaper than life' category, are precious stones, valuable historical decorations and ornaments, and all jewellery that must be simulated because of cost, and also because simplification usually looks better from the auditorium.

The business of exaggerating, of boldly defining small properties, may be the very essence of the property-maker's art, since it is called into play more often than any other factor – *all* properties demanding instant recognition by audiences if they have any significance in the dramatic development of the play. Some designers have developed the ability to exaggerate almost to the point of legerdemain; all have their own individual methods; and since almost any article imaginable may be used as a prop, obviously the treatment of all such objects cannot be described here. We can, however, give some likely examples.

PLATE 30   ALIX
STONE

Worthy (Basil
Hoskins) in **Virtue
in Danger,** directed
by Wendy Toye in
1963.

[31]

[32]

PLATE 32   ALIX STONE

Hostess and other characters in
The Taming of the Shrew, directed
by John Barton and Peter Hall in 1960.

50

PLATE 31 SOPHIE
FEYDOROVITCH (left)

Costumes for Moira Shearer,
Margot Fonteyn and Pamela
May in **Symphonic Variations**,
choreographer Frederick
Ashton, in 1946.

[33]

PLATE 33
ALIX STONE

Peachum (Harold
Blackburn) in **The
Beggar's Opera**,
directed by Colin
Graham in 1963.

Stock.
?

Cap [illegible] hat.

[35]

PLATE 34   ALIX STONE

Sly (Jack McGowan) in **The Taming of the Shrew,** directed by John Barton and Peter Hall in 1960.

PLATE 35   MOTLEY

Whores in **The Rake's Progress,** directed by Glen Byam Shaw in 1962.

[36]

[37]

PLATES 36, 37 MOTLEY

The Roaring Boy and Nick (Raymund)
Herincx) in **The Rake's Progress,**
directed by Glen Byam Shaw in 1962.

[38]

PLATE 38   MOTLEY

Mother Goose (Edith Coates) in
The Rake's Progress, directed by
Glen Byam Shaw in 1962.

[39]

[40]

PLATE 39   ALAN TAGG

Ellen (Elizabeth Fretwell) in **Peter Grimes,** directed by Basil Coleman in 1963. A simple sketch which shows the designer's sensitivity to the tender relationship between two characters helpful to the director and performers.

PLATE 40   MOTLEY

Naomi in **Noah,** directed by Michel St Denis in 1935. The costume design is rather dependent on the actress having a good figure. It was made of matt rayon jersey painted with a snakeskin design.

[41]

[42]

[43]

PLATE 41   MOTLEY

The lion in **Noah,** directed by Michel
St Denis in 1935. The mask was made
of papier maché and the mane of felt
strips. The animal-like effect was
dependent mainly on the head and
paws because human limb joints do
not correspond to those of an animal.

PLATE 42   MOTLEY

Black dog in **The Witch of Edmonton,**
directed by Michel St Denis in 1936.
The part was played by a dancer
who was able by his movement to
give a realistic impression of a dog.

PLATE 43   MOTLEY

Children in **Miss Liberty,** directed by
Moss Hart in 1949. Designing for
children is difficult, but by creating
character one can avoid sweetness
and sentimentality.

MARTY. AC

MOTLEY. 64.

[44]

58

[45]

PLATE 44   MOTLEY

Marty (Marie Collier) in **The Makropoulos Case**,
directed by John Blatchley in 1964.

PLATE 45   CECIL BEATON

Marguerite (Margot Fonteyn) in **Marguerite and
Armand,** choreographer Frederick Ashton
in 1963

[46]

[47]

PATIENCE

PINK TICKING:
WHITE EYELET
FLOWERS
STRAW BONNET
KERCHIEF
FLOWERED COTTON P
(unruly)

WIG
HAIR PIECE

STRAW
WITH
FLOWER
KERC

SLIPPERS

[48]

[49]

[50]

[51]

[52]

[53]

PLATES 49, 50, 51   RICHARD NEGRI

Oldest Troll (Russell Hunter), Bride's
Father (Fulton Mackay), and Troll
King (Esmond Knight) in **Peer Gynt,**
directed by Michael Elliot in 1962.
Though the heads on plates 49 and
51 are caricatured, the sketches are
beautifully clear and simple, and the
shapes of the bodies are full of
character and achievable.

PLATE 52   ROBERT O'HEARN

Ethiopian in **Aida,** directed by
Nathaniel Merril in 1963. This is a
case when the physique of the actor
is all important. If he is weedy, the
costume will not get the desired effect.

PLATE 53   MOTLEY

Character in **The Heretic,** directed by
Morris West with Joseph O'Connor in
1970.

[54]

PLATE 54   ALAN TAGG

Peter Grimes (Ronald Dowd), in **Peter Grimes** directed by Basil Coleman, in 1963.

PLATE 55
PETER WEXLER

Gabriel in a nativity play produced in a New York church in 1961.

[55]

6: THE MAKING OF STAGE AND COSTUME PROPERTIES

Let us suppose that you are given a property plot which includes a knife, a pistol, a watch and chain, a lorgnette case, a hand mirror and that weird miscellany of articles found in a woman's purse.

KNIFE   It is apparent that most knives, excepting perhaps that ferocious American weapon called the Bowie, will have inconsiderable significance when gripped by a relatively small fist in the reaches of a modern stage. Knife-wielders, moreover, seldom tarry in their attacks; a swift draw and lunge usually suffice for action; audiences are often left to wonder what sort of weapon was used, and sometimes to wonder if any weapon was used at all. Yet, by even subtly exaggerating the size of handle and blade, the prop-maker can usually remove all doubt. Let us presume that your handle is made to project beyond the tightly clenched fist, that it is ornamented in some eye-compelling manner, and that the blade is either highly polished, or treated with a metallic paint that will glitter wickedly in the light – if these things are done, and the actor holds the knife so that the broad side of the blade is exposed to the audience, few among the viewers will doubt that this is a theoretically lethal object.

PISTOL   Pistols are a more difficult matter. A lady bent upon murder, for example, may be expected to carry a diminutive weapon; a large calibre pistol would make her appear more ludicrous than deadly. But small arms can be specially 'blued' in gunsmiths' shops, or polished to a deadly sheen. Period weapons usually have mountings which readily adapt themselves to exaggeration, and the tone or colour of the weapon can contrast with the costume of the actor.

WATCH   Time-pieces are tricky; some exaggeration is possible, but none but a comic character will dare display an out-sized 'turnip' in this wrist-watch age, and here again the prop-maker must rely upon high polish as a means of catching the beholder's eye. You will have greater latitude in the matter of watch-chains. For some reason probably understood only by experts on the subject of optical illusion, a heavy watch-chain will often fail to elicit laughter where an over-sized time-piece will not.

LORGNETTE CASE   A lorgnette case is not a readily identifiable object, such optical aids not being standard female equipment in this or any age, and if you enlarge the proportions of the case merely to establish the fact that the lady is carrying a lorgnette, the audience may come to expect that the actress will presently haul a large pair of binoculars out of the box. We have solved the problem, or so we like to think, by bejewelling cases, by making them of brightly coloured leather, or by adding somewhat enlarged crests or monograms to the material used. Perhaps we did not make the presence of the case entirely intelligible, but we believed we cushioned the shock for audiences who would suddenly see a stage dowager whip out a set of glasses-on-a-stick and level it like a weapon at the world.

MIRROR   Mirrors are unequivocal things; stared into, they speak for themselves. But the back of a looking-glass seen by an audience may tell a different story. Not that any playgoer, however far from the stage, will doubt that an actress is peering at her own reflection – the act of any girl looking into a mirror is a gesture that must be recognizable on Mars – but the back of a mirror can certainly help the designer to delineate character; one can often tell a great deal about a personal object's owner by the object itself. Plain girls may not necessarily have plain hand mirrors, but many poor girls do, and a looking-glass with a backing of nondescript material or unadorned wood may speak quite eloquently of reduced financial circumstances. By the same token, a mirror embellished with jewels, gilded floral patterns, or any form of exaggerated decoration within reason and the range of the property-maker's craft, can fairly shriek of affluence. Wherever possible, the face of a mirror should be that of a real mirror. If it causes too much distraction by reflecting stage lights, its angle should be changed so that the audience will not see it. The only alternative is to dull the surface, to the least degree necessary, either by spraying it with emulsion glaze or black or dark grey emulsion paint, or by rubbing the surface lightly with soap.

CONTENTS   The contents of a woman's hand-bag often evoke mirth of the sort known as a
OF PURSE   'sight laugh' in the theatre, and any designer can have a 'field day' with the assortment of articles that may be turned out of a purse. We have used out-sized powder puffs and compacts, lip-stick containers large as big game ammunition, and no one has questioned their plausibility – probably because almost anything small enough to carry *might* be found in a modern woman's carry-all. And you can tell a great deal about a woman's station in life, and her character – or lack of it – by the outward appearance of her bag.

EMBELLISHING   The aforementioned articles are fairly typical of a property plot; most of them can
THE PROP   be purchased from readily available stocks. Costume houses usually employ experienced shoppers who keep files on source materials, especially of items frequently used, but you will have to search out the majority of articles for yourself, and junkshops of all

FIG 11
Necklace Chain

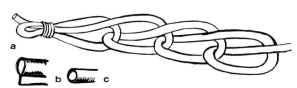

a Heavy chains can be made from rubber draught excluders, rubber or plastic tubing, or electric wire; the loops are pulled through each other like knitting, and painted with gold or silver paint.

b Section of draught excluder

c Tubing

kinds are happy hunting grounds for designers. You need not make the large watch chain mentioned; you merely purchase one made for a large time-piece, and attach it to a smaller one; and lorgnette cases, compacts, pistols and mirrors are easy to come by. These (the lethal hardware excepted) may be embellished in many ways. A floral pattern may be made with simulated jewels or motifs fashioned of braid, thus achieving 'relief' designs which may be secured by strong adhesives, such as the milk liquids or vegetable paste glues now available for commercial purposes. If the property is to undergo rough usage, re-inforce the glues by using wire, thread or staples as the case may allow. We have found that one of the most useful braids for such purposes is a narrow, tubular braid made of horsehair, available in many shades, with metallic threads interwoven. In fashioning the designs, especially in small pieces, it will be helpful if you make your motifs as symmetrical as possible; the more symmetry, the more readily identifiable the design.

As we have said, resident theatrical companies usually employ their own property men, but they usually have neither time nor training for making the more elaborate props, and an outside specialist is often called in when the plot demands articles which cannot be purchased or easily adapted, or simply made in the theatre workshop. Weaponry, aside from conventional modern armament, is frequently left to the costume designer-property-maker, as are shields, baldrics, banners and other items which require research, special designing and skilled workmanship.

CROWNS　　Crowns are among the most difficult of all properties to simulate properly – if one judges by the royal crests with which most stage monarchs are bedecked. We have often wondered if the sins of theatrical crown makers are not as grave, in their way, as were those of some of the real-life men and women who wore them. Of the bad ones available, almost all are too heavy for comfort, and even those which are synthetized usually

FIG 12

a Crown shape flat

b Shape made with crown

c As worn and decorated

a

b

c

run to cumbersome weight. We have worked out a comparatively painless formula for making crowns which have an authentic look, of either sized felt, 'Celastic' or papier maché, although the latter lacks durability if lightly made.

We first determine the circumference of the crown desired, and then draw the design upon any sort of strong paper. The pattern should be drawn flat, and with as much symmetry as possible, and you should allow for a lap-over when the circle is finally closed. A pattern cut from a better grade felt can be dipped or painted with 'size' or 'sizing' (a form of glue soluble in liquid – hot water, preferably). By bending the pattern into shape, when wet, your crown will dry rigid, and will maintain its shape through a reasonable amount of hard usage. Jewels or other ornaments can be fixed in place by strips of sized felt put on after the crown has dried, and metallic paint sprays lose none of their validity on sized felt. It is very important to fit the crown in its very early stages, to make sure that the shape and proportions suit the wearer, as nothing is more ridiculous than an ill-fitting, unbecoming crown. It is also a good idea, after the crown is finished and painted, to glue on some highlights of gold foil paper, which will add greatly to the metallic effect.

USING CELASTIC   Which brings us to a substance called 'Celastic', a wonderfully light, durable and rather expensive material. The fabric itself somewhat resembles heavy wall paper (it comes in several degrees of thickness) and, when saturated with a rather evil-smelling solution, also sold by the retailers of this product, can be used to simulate anything from an ornamental clock case to a battleship actually weighing no more than some of the smaller component parts of a real war craft.

We made crowns (and helmets) worn in Sir Laurence Olivier's Broadway production of *Becket* out of this material, slapping bits of it on, wringing wet with the solution, over an elaborately modelled base of clay. We used a clay sold under the trade name, 'Plasticine', but any soft, easily worked, non-hardening clay would have done well for the relief, since even the kinds advertised as non-hardening will 'cool' or stiffen enough after a few minutes so that they hold their shape under a covering of oil, vaseline or a special parting agent, also sold by the retailers, and also expensive. Aluminium foil is applied over the parting agent, carefully pressed in so that the design will 'carry', and the wet Celastic should then be added. It dries in a reasonably short time, and when dried, comes easily away from the foil and clay beneath. It somehow achieves an astonishing toughness in drying. As a small boy, the son of one of us paddled a canoe made of Celastic through the waves along the Connecticut shore, and the wooden outrigger of the small craft weighed several times as much as the body of the boat.

Celastic takes almost all kinds of paint very well, as does heavier papier maché, but lends itself to certain colour effects more readily than the paper. Metallic sprays, if 'over-rubbed' with paints in olive green, black or khaki shades, give the material a worn and tarnished look, almost unbelievably authentic. Celastic, however, is not good for extremely small properties; tiny bits of the material stick to even the most skilful fingers and become unmanageable once the solution begins to dry. Such accessories as bracelets, large earrings, etc., can be fabricated without great difficulty, and in all properties in which weight is a factor, the material is invaluable to the designer.

MASKS   We have made many masks of Celastic, and this may be a good place to say a few words about masks in general. If you are asked to make a mask that is an exact representation of an actor, you had better be adept indeed at modelling, but if you are not, you can fall back upon the technique used in making death masks of the great for hundreds of years. The death mask approach involves piling wet plaster on the face, which is not very pleasant for a living person. So, as an alternative, you grease the face thoroughly and use plaster-impregnated surgical bandage, which can be laid on in strips, leaving the nostrils free to allow breathing. The hair should be protected by a towel. When the bandage has dried, it can be removed as a whole without difficulty. Thereafter you can add layers of plaster to the outside to strengthen it. You then thoroughly grease the inside of this rough cast, dump wet plaster into it, and when that plaster has dried, remove the outer layer with careful blows from a hammer.

If all goes well, you will have an expert cast of the subject's face, complete even to blemishes. But it takes a bold hand and a sure one to work in this medium, and we ourselves prefer the greater labour involved in making a clay facsimile of features, over which wet Celastic can be applied. Some police departments have developed easier methods of *moulage*, using rubber-based materials which, however, are rather closely guarded secrets, and are rarely used commercially.

Character masks that bear no particular resemblance to humans are easier to design, and the element of hazard is certainly reduced; but there is a considerable amount of labour involved in making these, also, as eyes and mouth must fit with those of the actors wearing them. In the musical, *Kwamina*, we had to produce a number of symbolical African tribal masks, larger than shoulder-to-knee length shields. It would have been impossible to make the basic models of clay; for one thing, we could not manipulate that much damp earth all at once, and even clays warranted to be 'non-hardening' lose malleability through hours of exposure to air and light. We resorted to the use of cardboard strips, bent roughly into shape around an empty barrel, laid a covering of papier maché over the framework, used clay for lips, noses and brows, and then added a final 'skin' of Celastic, or a latex compound.

Papier maché work is done best in a negative mould, which should be greased well, with vaseline. Soak some newspaper or any soft coloured paper in water and tear it into pieces about three inches square. Make some cold water paste, such as is used by paper hangers, spread this thinly on both sides of pieces of the paper and press them into the mould, making sure there are no air bubbles, and no surplus paste. When the whole surface is covered, repeat the process with the paper (by using two colours you can see to make the layers fairly even). Next add a layer of pieces of tarlatan muslin, also cut into small squares and pasted, then another two layers of the coloured paper, finishing off with another of tarlatan; more layers can be added if a very strong mould is needed. Allow the result to dry until it is quite hard, then remove it from the mould, cut and trim the edges and bind them with pasted strips of paper or tarlatan. The surface can be rubbed down with fine sandpaper, and painted with shellac, to act as a filler, and after that the model can be painted with whatever kind of paint is most suitable.

On one occasion, in Trinidad, we were called upon to make two enormous masks – the traditional masks of Comedy and Tragedy – which were to be transported by means of long poles, and would have to withstand hard usage. There was no Celastic available, and if we had used enough layers of papier maché to make them durable, we doubt that any single Trinidadian could have carried one of them. We finally made them resemble masks carved from gigantic coconuts – complete with palm-leaf hair – and to do so we used raffia and fibre matting woven across the glad and sad mouths of Comedy and Tragedy, which were fashioned of strong wire.

USING WOOD   Every property-maker must do some work in wood, although it can rarely be termed the designer's friend. Wood splinters and breaks, and if it runs to size, any property made from anything other than balsa must also run to weight. It has, moreover, when painted to look like something else, a maddening tendency to look like nothing except wood painted to look like something else. But until someone devises some lighter material for making such objects as spears and lances and staves, designers and actors must put up with it.

If you are called upon to provide poles or pike-staffs for practical use, test them well: remember that staves which must be very long will waver, in fact become almost unmanageable, unless they are thick enough to support gracefully their own height. Poles over ten feet in length should be at least one inch in diameter. Aluminium or steel tubing can be thinner in proportion to its length than wood, and does not weigh much more; it serves very well and will take most kinds of paint. If you require finials or top pieces, you can reduce the weight by making them of Celastic, and if you must paint wood and wish it to look worn and weathered, there are a number of quick-drying alcohol stains – they come in olive green, silver-blue, mahogany and other natural shades – which can be quickly and easily applied with a sponge.

FOAM RUBBER   Foam rubber is a very useful substance, which can be carved and cut with a sharp knife or scissors, into bold shapes for epaulets or large pieces of decoration, or to build up on hard surfaces. It takes dye, paint or metallic paint, and if mounted on a firm felt or canvas is strong, durable and very lightweight.

JEWELLERY   Jewellery is the most highly personalized of all costume accessories, and even if considerable exaggeration is made possible by a play script that conveniently includes vulgar and ostentatious characters, jewels must be relatively small articles. Good jewellers' 'fakes' are prohibitive in cost, and although you may purchase outrageously large imitation diamonds and other precious stones, these have limited uses, and in most cases you will have to provide the settings yourself. We have found that several small imitation diamonds, tightly glued together, will seem one large stone, if ingeniously mounted, and several strings of smallish Woolworth pearls bound together may give

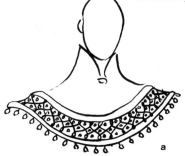

a   b   c

the look of one large necklace. Elastic braid interwoven with metallic thread makes a good setting for smaller 'jewels', and large pieces may be mounted upon felt. Both materials react well to either gold or silver paint sprays.

Much of property jewellery making is a matter of special design. We have known exceptionally skilled persons who have used the theatre as a sort of back door into the generally lucrative field of costume jewellery design and manufacture, or who have made it a remunerative marginal business while still employed in the theatre. The craftsmen who create expensive jewellery are themselves artists, and work from carefully drawn designs. If you are working with false stones and simulated gold and silver, no one will expect you to be another Cellini, but your ornaments should follow a recognizable pattern, which will require work at the drawing-board, and probably involve research also. Slip-shod design or methods will certainly detract from your chances of making an imitated article look real.

As a rather good example of special design, in the production of *Lorenzo* we were required to make several articles of tawdry jewellery which, in the play, were used by actors who themselves portrayed a company of strolling players. Among the garish ornaments was a so-called 'Cleopatra' necklace, which had to show signs of hard wear. We began by making a paper pattern of the familiar cowl shape, and then cut the base from turquoise felt. We bought an old bamboo window blind in a second-hand furniture store, and ripped off the tubes in which the pull cords of the blind were housed. We glued two inch pieces of the tubes vertically on the felt, interspersed with

FIG 13 Jewellery

a Collar: thick felt base (black or whatever colour suits the costume); heavy braid edge, either metallic or embossed (black, grey or brown); criss-cross design in gold paint, twisted metal or lurex cord, with paper clip studs and painted wooden beads at the edge.

b Brooch: basic shape cut in tailor's canvas, covered with smooth metallic cloth; heart an imitation crystal, or two or three layers of felt with gold or sequins; feather shapes outlined with lurex cord; imitation pearls at the edges.

c Bracelet: felt base painted gold or silver and covered with perspex; edge and decoration made from two thicknesses of plastic-covered electric wire painted gold.

d Brooch: large square imitation crystal mounted on felt; scroll design made from plastic-covered electric wire.

e Pendant: oval ring made of very fine cane plaited; star shape of thin balsa wood mounted on canvas and covered with silver foil paper, slightly tooled; silver beads at tips; pearls between arms of the star and in the centre.

f Pendant: very strong canvas plate in centre; the rest made from fine plastic-covered electric wire, pulled through hole in the centre of the plate.

g and **h** Rings: made from lurex cord, pearls and beads.

d   e   f   g

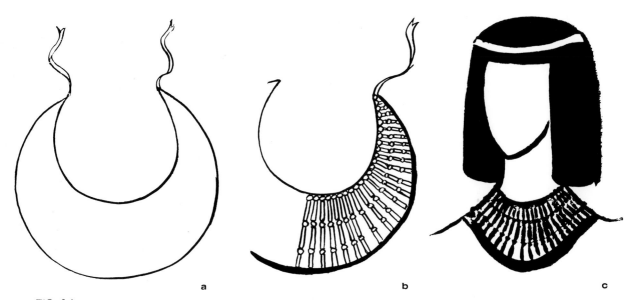

FIG 14

**Cleopatra's
Necklace**

a felt base

b Decorated with
bamboo sticks and
beads

c As worn

some of the wooden beads with which the blind was also ornamented. We sprayed the
bits of tube with gold paint, painted the wooden beads crimson, man-handled the
necklace into a semblance of age, and finally 'broke' it down by spraying it with
black paint, which gave it a dingy appearance without entirely disguising either the
original design or the bold colours in which it had been made.

The property-maker may be asked to create fanciful military decorations, and you
may have fun with these, since they need not 'hew' close to reality. *We Take The Town*
(see plate 46) was a musical which fell somewhat short of its backers' expectations – and
fell short of ever opening on Broadway, too – but visually it was a designer's holiday.
In the production, an actor playing a Mexican dictator was supposed to wear more
medals than any one man could ever carry. We made them of felt, ribbon, wire, red,
blue and white sequins, braids, simulated pearls, electric cord, old beads, and other
odds and ends out of a box in which we had been storing work-room remnants for years.
They looked real enough, and brought forth the desired amount of laughter, but, on
second thoughts, perhaps the production *was not* exactly a holiday, because an incredible
amount of work went into fashioning that decorative hodge-podge. Of the fifty or
more absurd orders that gleamed on the actor's chest, almost every one was made
from a separate design.

DECORATIONS   There are, of course, military orders and civic decorations which are actually too
small for effective use on the stage, and if the play-script demands reality, the designer
will be hard put to make such things stand out. We advise backing them in felt
without *too* much exaggeration of the medal's outline, giving it the *emphasized* look of
an outlined alphabetical letter. And if small metal objects cannot be burnished into
an eye-catching shimmer, one of the brighter metallic paints will usually have the
desired effect.

TOOLS TO USE.   A complete list of property-making materials would probably be impossible by definition, but we can supply a sort of working hypothesis. Suppose *you* were called upon, as we once were, to go to a far place which had sorely limited resources, and design costumes and props for a production still in the writing stage, with almost any sort of a property possibility once the script has been completed. What materials would you take along?

You would want the basic tools of the designer: paints, brushes, drawing-paper and cardboard for sketches, graph paper for detailed drawings, as well as stencil paper, a T-square, set square, compass and ruler, scissors, a sharp-edged cutting knife (Stanley trimming knife or a scalpel), and a pair of 'snips' that cut tin and wire and heavy cardboard. You would want Celastic, and the solution in which it is soaked, although papier maché might be used as a substitute if Celastic is not available; felt in as many colours as possible, metallic cloth, as wide a variety of braids as possible, needles, pins, strong linen thread, buttons, ribbons, latex and impact glues, bulk size, paint sprays (especially in black and khaki shades, for break-down purposes); ornamental tacks, curtain rings, beads, sequins, simulated pearls, and as great a variety as possible of light-weight metal ornaments. A staple-gun would also be useful.

Your luggage would resemble the pack of a trader setting out to barter with native tribes, and you would give customs' inspectors fits. But if you had all of these articles, and more, the chances are that the prop list would contain items you were not equipped to make. The chances are, also, that you would make them somehow, out of materials you would somehow manage to find.

7: FACTS ABOUT FABRICS

Mankind has been wearing clothing for many centuries – and often not very well. Legend tells us that the goddess Athena turned Arachne into a spider because the maiden wove a fabric surpassing anything that had come from Athena's loom, and if this were so, it probably marked one of the few occasions upon which an artisan was ever penalized for positive excellence. However, if Arachne had cut and sewn a garment of the stuff she made, Athena might not have been soured by envy. There may seem to be a touch of divinity in some of the 'miracle' fabrics produced today, but there is apt to be little of it in the making of a garment, and often, in the selection of material, no evidence of divinity at all.

It is said that Samuel Johnson was known to argue in private that the human body was never made to wear clothes, and to offer as conclusive proof the way he looked when clothed himself. Even at the risk of premature retirement, there are times when the costume designer is tempted to agree with Doctor Johnson, or at least wish alternatively that all men – and most women – might be dressed in that most adaptable of all fabrics, wool jersey.

USING WOOL JERSEY

The material of which a costume is made is as important as the cut or fit of the garment; good amateur productions look better if materials are wisely chosen, bad professional productions may appear a great deal worse if they are not. In period costume, wool jersey is indeed the boon and solace of the harassed designer, the very *beau ideal* of fabrics. Its weight is inconsiderable in comparison to its strength, it comes in a wide variety of colours and surface textures, it drapes and folds admirably, it can be made to fit even the most fit-resistant of bodies, and if this last may seem to be the same general principle upon which sausages are stuffed, so be it: wool jersey is tough also. It is a venerable material, with royal associations; the silken hose of Queen Elizabeth I were made from the same tight, cunning stitch that, adapted to machinery, now produces wool jersey in vast quantities. There is only one thing wrong with it from the theatrical standpoint, and that single deficiency may obviate against its use: wool jersey is expensive, beyond the reach, so far as mass use is concerned, of the modest production budget.

YOUR PRODUCTION

We have said before that all designers are figuratively the slaves of production budgets, and even at the risk of belabouring the point, we advise newcomers in the profession to make haste slowly when spending the backer's money.

In women's costumes, rayon jersey can be an acceptable cheaper substitute for wool jersey, but this hybrid fabric often does not look well on men. As an alternative in period costume, we have often dressed male performers in upholstery materials of the sort sold in most **department** stores. They are enormously wide, are made in a magnificent range of colours and designs, and can be obtained with either rough or smooth surfaces.

Substitutes can – or perhaps we had better say *must* – be found for most expensive or impracticable materials. During our working lifetime, there has been an increasing tendency to avoid the use of conventional silks and velvets in theatrical costume. As we have stated, a Motley production of *Hamlet* simulated brocades by painting one of the cheapest of all available materials, scenery canvas. The critics approved, and the production *did* represent our genuine feeling of revolt against the trite and the hackneyed in period stage wear, but we had little choice in the matter, anyway; there simply was not enough in that particular budget with which to purchase more costly materials.

In period costumes, we have avoided as far as possible the use of soft machine-made satins and velvets, rayon taffetas and brocades, which give no feeling of period, and contrive to lend clothing made of them a look of mere 'fancy dress' rather than the affect of reality required.

VELVET Velvet, which has been described as the cloth of kings and courtiers and the ultimate repository of all the dust motes and microbes in the community, fortunately has a poor cousin. Known to the trade as 'Velveteen', this hardy impostor of fabrics may, under proper circumstances, give a fairly convincing imitation of raiment royal. It is, of course, made of cotton, but given the 'body' it lacks – that is, an inner lining of cotton felt or tailors' canvas – velveteen wears well, and looks well too. It is sold in a wide assortment of colours, can be easily dyed and reacts splendidly to light. One exception, however, should be noted: we have never been able to find an effective *black* velveteen. Almost all stage light tends to turn existing specimens a murky grey colour, and if an intense and honest black is desired, genuine velvet must be used – not a soft one, but one with plenty of body, some stiffness and short pile.

SATIN If there is any worthy substitute for satin, we have not yet encountered it. Our prejudice against the modern 'soft' satins is based, in large part, upon the fact that they had not been invented when that noble cloth was widely worn by men as well as women. However, most fabric stores now stock a cotton-backed satin which bears a resemblance to the stiff, hand-produced fabric of the past.

SYNTHETIC FABRICS If synthetic fabrics are to be used, they must be selected very carefully. They are seldom as satisfactory as natural cloth, but some of the recent products are good. Those that are thin, sleazy, and floppy should be studiously avoided. Look for weight, for fabric that folds and shapes well. Some of the more useful synthetic fabrics are nylon net and organza, which do not crush; heavy, rough rayon jersey; and heavy furnishing fabrics, such as dull satin, velvet, ottoman, and linen. The cotton blends and some of the wool and nylon blends can be very satisfactory. Good quality synthetic fur fabric can be useful, though expensive. Most rayon will dye well, and the colour can be easily removed from it.

**PERIOD
COSTUMES**   The designing and making of a successful period costume may be said to be figuratively a wedding between illusion and reality, a compromise between beautiful fancy
and less lovely fact. But the designer is indebted both to history and to the great
variety of materials which can, so to speak, make that history come alive. Out of
rough wools and tweeds, linens, and even the lowly hessian (now manufactured in
many colours) something close to a maximum in the way of reality may be achieved.
The garb of workers and peasants throughout the ages had usually a dignity which in
itself had a kind of beauty; the materials named above were more or less what they
did wear, and are what they should wear when portrayed on the modern stage.
Ironically, however, expensive raw silk gives a splendidly home-spun look almost
impossible to duplicate among modern materials.

**DESIGNING
FINERY**   Finery is a somewhat different matter, but designers will do well to bear in mind
that sartorial richness was not always expressed in terms of velvet and satin and ermine
and silk. Holbein and other court painters depicted their subjects as though dressed
for a bright Sunday, seldom for the Monday that must inevitably follow even in the
lives of kings. Monarchs such as England's Henry VII dressed almost as workmen did,
in unofficial moments, and although the frugal Henry may have been an extreme
exception, most great lords had their 'second best'; probably only by their jewels
could you have told them from the ranks of a woollen or linen clad yeomanry.

**PRODUCING THE
IDEAL COSTUME**   The ideal costume, from the designer's standpoint, is one that looks well, fits well,
wears well, and, above all, seeks to delineate clearly the character which the actor
portrays. In the view of the director – either a long view or a short one, depending
upon where one sits – the ideal costume should embody all those qualities, cost as
little as possible, and, if possible, wear for ever. The actor asks only that his clothes
look and fit well and afford him freedom of movement, and not be too heavy, although
he may *hope* that they will make him look beautiful, too. Unfortunately, there are
no all-inclusive materials with which these optimistic specifications can be met, nor
are there likely to be any, barring miracles of a sort not wrought in textile laboratories.
For whatever it may be worth as a commentary upon man's ingenuity – or lack of it –
we offer the opinion that, if we were limited to the choice of a single material with
which to work, the choice might well be linen – the oldest textile known to history.
     The Spanish *conquistador*, Francisco Pizarro, came to Peru wearing silks and jewels,
and marvelled at the beauty of the natives' clothing. The costumes he saw added to
his conviction that the Incas were fabulously wealthy people, although their dress was
actually made of simple stuff – linen and cotton – woven by native artisans, and gaily
coloured with dyes which they also produced. This is probably an extreme example
of how effective design may be, for Pizarro put most of the Incas to the sword, but
the point is, the designs were *good*, and the artists worked with what they had.
     The lines of their cotton garments were simple, as they should be. Cotton has a
great variety of uses, but plain cotton is still the stuff of which winding sheets are made
and the cloth of slaves, and even in its most grandiose dyed or printed states, it crushes
and wrinkles and lacks any semblance of regality when folded or draped.
     Wool, on the other hand, folds and drapes beautifully, adapts itself extremely well

to fitting, and usually comes in greater widths than the less expensive but narrower synthetic fabrics. Silk is still the aristocrat of materials, as it has been since its first introduction to the western world. Machine-made raw silk, previously mentioned, has a hand-woven look that makes it seem a truly fabulous fabric to the period designer. Pure silk taffeta is excellent for simulating eighteenth-century costumes; Otterman, a heavy ribbed silk, is impressive when additional weight is required in a garment; silk crêpe drapes admirably, fits well, and is recommended for costumes worn by dancers, because it has amazing elasticity yet also clings to the human body.

Chiffon, a product of comparatively modern times, is *not* recommended for use except in modern costume, for the reason that no matter what one does to it, it still manages to look somehow like the newcomer among fabrics that it is.

A good way to represent heavy leather garments is to use thick floor felt, treat the surface by rubbing it hard all over with moist yellow soap, and then paint or spray to give age and texture. The thinner felts do not make up very well as the surface is so flat, but they make a good backing or lining. Incidentally, it often takes less time to dye fabrics to the exact colours that you want, than to shop for them, as sometimes the right combination of the colour and texture are almost impossible to find.

Few materials are truly cheap, in the sense that our fathers knew economy. It is one of the mysteries of our modern affluent society that, although the production of textiles constantly soars to meet the demands of ever increasing consumption, the resultant competition somehow fails to force the price of fabrics down. The present cost structure seems to be based upon the assumption that the more you have of something, the more you can get for it; and if there are economists who can explain this mercantile phenomenon, we doubt that they could do so to the satisfaction of struggling theatrical producers. Many of the professionals in the field admit to considerable discouragement, and hard-pressed amateurs are said to be using some unlikely materials indeed. To these, let us again emphasize that scenery canvas and unbleached calico are still reasonably cheap, and so, relatively speaking, is paint. We would certainly have recourse to them, as an alternative to using sleazy fabrics, or materials which we knew to be historically wrong.

8: CUTTING AND FITTING PERIOD COSTUMES

The unmistakable silhouette of a period costume (see pages 2-3, 142-3 of this book) can only be achieved by padding, corseting and the correct cut.

Men's period costumes have much more sloping shoulders than we are used to; in addition the chest is usually more rounded, the seat more protruding and the calves of the legs fuller. We can see these differences in contemporary pictures throughout the centuries; to some extent, of course, the conventions of painting are responsible, but riding, archery and other activities of the times almost certainly developed different sets of muscles to those developed by modern life.

PADDING   Padding, which should be made separately for an actor to wear under the costume, can do much to provide the characteristic shape of a period. It can also help to indicate character. The human body may become distorted by age, fat or deformity: in old age the head sinks into the shoulders, the back rounds, the knees and elbow joints sometimes become enlarged; fatness also affects the length of the neck, and character is often revealed by the way in which a man's stomach protrudes or by the enlargement or misplacement of a woman's breasts, hips or seat; minor character-revealing deformities can frequently be shown by asymmetrical padding. Some occupations, too, affect the figure: coal miners become thick through the shoulders, labourers are generally more heavily built than actors, athletes more broad-shouldered, accountants and clerks develop stoops and round shoulders. All of which, of course, demands from the designer a thorough knowledge of anatomy and an acute power of observation.

The actual making of padding requires great skill and care. It is first necessary to construct a well-fitting calico garment as a foundation for whatever part of the body or limbs is to be padded. The distortion should then be built up bit by bit with layers of cotton wadding, each of which is firmly stitched to the foundation. When the desired shape seems to have been achieved it should be tried on *underneath* a costume, for only then is it possible to judge size and proportion accurately. Once finished, the padding needs to be made very firm – which means a great deal of stabbing through to the foundation with a long needle and strong thread. The final stage is to cover the wadding with a soft material such as soft muslin or very thin unbleached calico which will not spoil the details of the shape; a coarser material will tend to make it 'cornery'.

It is important that the shapes of muscles should be clearly formed, especially in the case of chest and shoulder padding which has to be worn under a shirt or other thin garment. For small paddings foam rubber can be substituted for wadding; it is easier to handle and lighter to wear, and can be easily shaved and trimmed into shape.

Women's period costumes, from the fifteenth century onwards, nearly always need corsets, the shapes of which vary from age to age (see *Corsets and Crinolines* by Norah

Waugh, Batsford). The same effect cannot be obtained by boning the dresses, nor can a padded costume replace a padding worn under a costume; all padding must seem to be part of the body and the costume must be made to fit that body.

SEAMS   One of the most important differences between the costumes of various periods is the placing of seams. Standards of beauty, elegance and attraction have changed through the centuries, and seams were, and are, carefully placed to enhance the kind of figure fashionable at a given time. In the 1950s, for example, very square shoulders and a flat chest and back were considered fashionable in a man; the shoulder seam of a coat was therefore placed on the top of the shoulder and the side seam near the middle of the side. In Regency days, on the other hand, fashion demanded a more sloping shoulder and a pouter-pigeon chest, an effect which was achieved by placing the shoulder seam far back at an acute angle and the side seam further towards the rear of the coat.

FIG 15   **Paddings**

a To shorten neck and thicken shoulders to give age

b Aggressive business man

c Very gross elderly man

d Soft professional type of elderly man

e Sedentary character such as clerk or watchmaker

f Middle-aged heavy man for period costume

g Athletic type of man

h Seat padding to give shape to late nineteenth century or early twentieth century woman's skirts

i Plump middle-aged woman

j Blowzy middle-aged or elderly woman

k Very fat woman

l 'Muscle' padding to be worn under shirt; this kind is better based on a flexible garment such as a vest or jersey

m Suitable for most period costumes for young men

n Asymmetrical padding for deformed character

o Burly middle-aged man

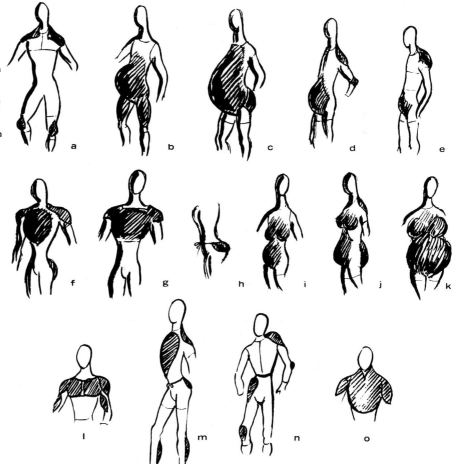

CUTTING THE
AUTHENTIC
COSTUME

As we said earlier, a professional cutter – who is often a real artist in his own field – may be reluctant to follow authentic period cut, partly because he fears the actor may find it uncomfortable to wear and partly because he has been conditioned for years by people who cannot detach themselves from the conventions of modern times. Nevertheless authenticity is essential, and it is a very important part of the designer's work to get on good terms with the cutter, so that there can be a real collaboration between them over this.

The drawings on the following pages illustrate and explain the cutting of some typical costumes worn by men and women in different periods, from medieval times to the twentieth century.

An accepted practice among some of the less expensive costumiers is to make all costumes fasten down the back – partly because it is easier to fit the front well if you do this and 'the back will not show so much'. But the result is to destroy all feeling of reality, especially if, as is so often the case, there is also a false fastening at the front. It is, therefore, as well to note on the costume sketch where the fastening should be placed, so that the cutter is aware of what you want before he cuts the fabric.

It is usually best to cut a garment first in unbleached calico and to fit this on the wearer, leaving the cutting of the more expensive material until you have obtained the correct shape. At the next stage, consider carefully how best to use the fabric's grain. Fabric on the cross hangs and stretches very differently from fabric on the straight, and in some cases the length of the cloth behaves very differently from the width. Make sure, too, that you have enough fabric; a good material is important, but it is better to use a cheap material like unbleached calico and have plenty of it, than to use silk and have to skimp.

ADJUSTING THE
COSTUME

At fittings the designer must be prepared to make radical adjustments. It often happens, for instance, that a woman's costume, designed originally with a high neck, proves unbecoming to a particular actress, and it would be better to change to a low or wide neck line. A designer, in fact, must be prepared to be flexible so long as changes can be made without loss of style or character. Major changes should, of course, be discussed with the director.

For amateurs and companies trying to build up their own wardrobe – often without a great deal of money – it is worth considering that certain 'basic' garments can be used in a number of different ways for the costumes of various periods. We have become more and more aware of the possibilities here over the years, and have therefore made this the subject of the next section.

Finally, we cannot emphasize enough the importance of studying costumes in museums, both in the exhibits of period clothes and in the paintings of the period.

PLATE 56
MOTLEY

Third robber in **The Snow Queen,** directed by Suria Magito and Michel St Denis in 1947. The tunic was made of heavy felt with the design appliquéd in thin felt. The wool trousers were painted with spots.

[58]

PLATE 57 MOTLEY

Sherlock Holmes (Fritz Weaver) in **Baker Street,**
directed by Harold Prince in 1965. Collection, Mr.
and Mrs. Alexander H. Cohen. Holmes' classic
coat was made of blue grey plaid wool; his suit of
black and deep blue wool. The beggar disguise,
portrayed at the right, consisted of a cape turned
up over the head, covered with a large ragged
black wool shawl.

PLATE 58 MOTLEY

Malcolm and Donalbane in **Macbeth,** American
Shakespeare Festival, Stratford, Connecticut,
1969. The costumes were made of heavy wool
and felt, and had padded shoulders.

PLATE 59 MOTLEY

Irene Adler (Inga Swenson) in **Baker Street,**
directed by Harold Prince in 1965. Irene Adler's
dress was made of pale grey crepe, embroidered
in grey chenille and iridescent sequins. She wore
a grey feather boa, grey velvet purse, grey parasol,
and eggshell gloves.

[59]

[57]

PLATE 60 MOTLEY

King John (Michael Horden), directed by George Devine in 1953. To be in keeping with the existing Renaissance set the basic costume was Elizabethan but had brilliantly coloured medieval additions. The doublet and hose were dark green, the cloak bright yellow and the crown gold.

PLATE 61 MOTLEY

Regan (Angela Baddeley) in **King Lear**, directed by Glen Byam Shaw in 1959. In an endeavour to avoid any specific period this costume was a simple underdress of matt rayon jersey, with a cloth tabard, an elaborate decorated collar and a crown. The sisters and their retinues were each identified by a specific colour.

[60]

KING LEAR.

REGAN

ANGELA BADDELEY

CEREMONIAL ROBES.

MOTLEY

[61]

[62]

[63]

[65]

[64]

PLATE 62   MOTLEY

Dancer in arrival of the girls in **Paint Your Wagon,** directed by Daniel Mann, choreography by Agnes DeMille, in 1951.

PLATE 63   MOTLEY

Gold rush number in **Paint Your Wagon,** directed by Daniel Mann, choreography by Agnes DeMille, in 1951.

PLATE 64   MOTLEY

Pancho Villa (Robert Preston) in **We Take the Town,** directed by Alex Segal in 1962. Pancho Villa's jacket was made of leather, his shirt was linen, leggings were leather. He wore an imported Mexican sombrero and a dark red and black poncho.

PLATE 65   MOTLEY

Ballet Revolution in **We Take the Town,** directed by Alex Segal in 1962. The ranchers in this scene wore black wool tights, leather leggings, and lightweight sombreros specially made for the dancers.

"PETER PAN"
CYRIL RITCHARD
AS
CAPTAIN HOOK

[67]

PLATE 66   MOTLEY

Captain Hook (Cyril Ritchard) in **Peter Pan,** directed by
Jerome Robbins in 1950. Collection, Mr. and Mrs. Alexander
H. Cohen. This brilliant red coat was made of velvet; the
jabot and cuffs of orange lace.

PLATE 67   MOTLEY

Harriet (Victoria de los Angeles) and Nancy (Rosalind Elias)
in **Martha,** a Metropolitan Opera production, staged by
Carl Elbert in 1961. Printed cotton dresses, lace and batiste
pantalets, striped cotton apron are the major elements in
these two costumes.

[68]

[69]

PLATE 68   MOTLEY

The Queen in **Martha**, a Metropolitan Opera
production, staged by Carl Elbert
in 1961. The Queen's habit was made of
black velvet. She also wore a black top hat
with plumes and veil.

PLATE 69   MOTLEY

Vendor at the Richmond Fair in **Martha,**
a Metropolitan Opera production, staged
by Carl Elbert in 1961. This peddler
wore a ragged wool coat and pants and a
tattered hat.

PLATE 70   MOTLEY

Ladies in the Queen's party in **Martha,**
a Metropolitan Opera production, staged
by Carl Elbert in 1961. These women were
wearing riding habits in all shades of
grey, as well as grey and black velvet
top hats.

[71]

PLATE 71   MOTLEY

Women singers in **Tovarich**, directed by Peter
Glenville in 1963.

PLATE 72 MOTLEY

Prince of Arragon in
**The Merchant of
Venice** (Colin
Jevons), directed by
Glen Byam Shaw in
1967. The production
was set in the
eighteenth century.
This character was
meant to look slightly
ridiculous and the
effect was created by
exaggerating the
shape and over-
decorating the
costume.

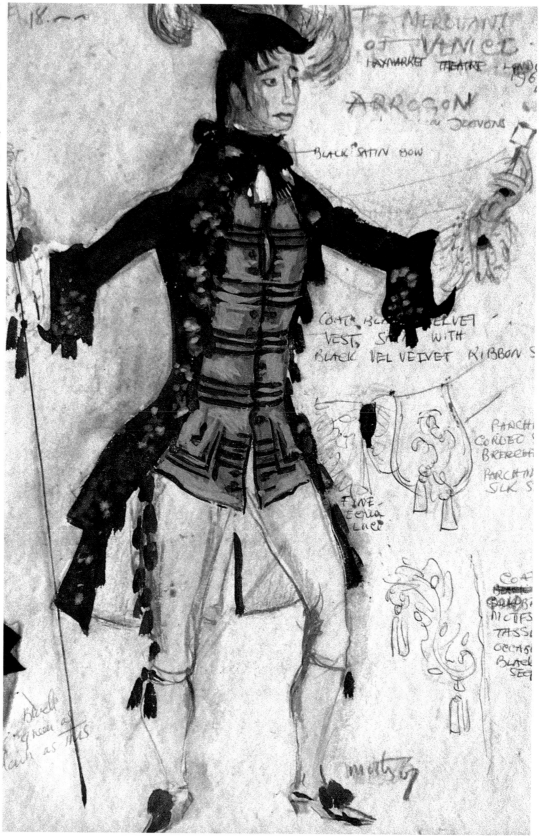

[72]

[73]

[74]

PLATE 73 MOTLEY

Wolf (Han Bergman) in **Lorenzo,** directed
by Arthur Penn in 1963. Over the tunic,
this costume was made of leather; under
the tunic this costume was wool. The
cloak was made of rough ragged wool.
Wolf wore thick wool tights, ragged suede
boots, and pieces of rusty and tattered
armour.

PLATE 74 MOTLEY

Pombo (Herb Edelman) in **Lorenzo,**
directed by Arthur Penn in 1963. Pombo's
leather jerkin was studded with rusty
gun metal studs. He wore a rough wool
tunic; a tattered rusty Georget helmet;
torn thick wool tights; a black leather
baldric, and shabby suede boots.

[75]

PLATE 75   DON FOOTE

Soldier in **The Athenian Touch,** directed by
Alex Palermo in 1964.

[76]

PLATE 76 PETER WEXLER

A pedant and Baptista in
Taming of the Shrew, directed by
Stuart Vaughn in 1963.

FIG 16   Medieval: man

a Basically a fitted tunic, sometimes parti-coloured, and wool tights—perhaps a striped leg.

b Various types of robe can be worn on top, with

c many different kinds of sleeve.

c and **d** The head-dress (a 'chaperone'), most easily made from wool jersey, is a hood with long pointed 'liripipe' and face hole; round the face hole is stitched a padded roll which is then worn on the head, the 'slittered' part of the hood hanging down from the top, and the liripipe across the neck.

e A simple hood sometimes worn under a hat.

f Examples of shoes, made of thick felt or wool jersey.

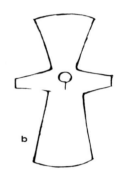

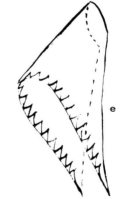

FIG 17 **Medieval:** woman

a and **b** Very simple basic shape
for underdress. If wide enough
material is used, this garment can
be cut flat for back and front
together; if not, a shoulder seam
is necessary.

c and **d** Various overdresses will
denote rank and character, and

e there are many varieties of
sleeve.

f and **g** The hair is nearly always
completely covered. A wimple is
worn with a face hole, the easiest
material for which is fine jersey
because this clings to the face.

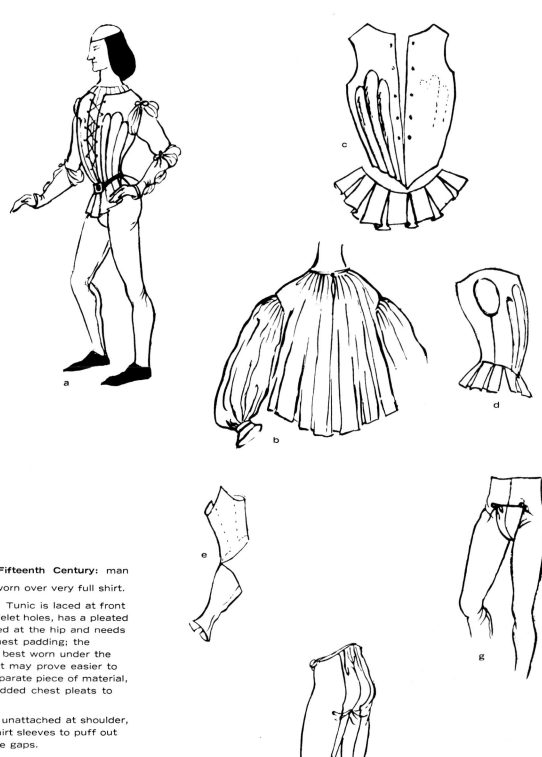

FIG 18 **Fifteenth Century:** man

a Tunic, worn over very full shirt.

b, c and **d** Tunic is laced at front through eyelet holes, has a pleated skirt divided at the hip and needs a lot of chest padding; the padding is best worn under the shirt, but it may prove easier to stitch a separate piece of material, making padded chest pleats to the tunic.

e Sleeves unattached at shoulder, allowing shirt sleeves to puff out through the gaps.

f Hose, which were not woven tights, at this period, but cut from woollen material.

g Codpiece in front, lined with canvas and tied up with lacing.

FIG 19 **Mid-Fifteenth Century:**
woman

a Dress of young girl; low, wide
neckline to sleeveless bodice, very
high waistline; worn over very full
shirt or blouse, skirt pleated or
gathered in all round; much
fullness in front also.

b Cutting pattern for bodice and
skirt.

c Cutting pattern for velvet
sleeve, in two parts.

d Hennan head-dress; tall,
pointed, embroidered hat; very
fine stiff muslin, organdie or
gauze, on wire frame.

a

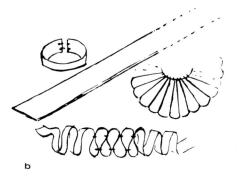

b

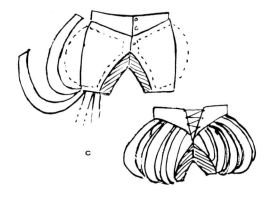

c

FIG 20   **End of Sixteenth Century:** man
a Doublet with slashing, full breeches
and ruffs.

b Method of making ruff: construct
linen neckband, fastening at back and
narrowing towards front; take long strip
of material the width you wish the ruff
to be from neckband to outer edge;
fold in pleats to width of neckband,
stitch pleats together on outer edge;
stitch close together on to top and
bottom of neckband in the centre of
pleats.

c Method of making full breeches: fitted
trunks with plain area inside thigh;
padding, covered with material which
you 'whisk' in strips so that padding
remains visible; strips should be backed
with felt or canvas.

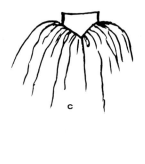

FIG 21　**Mid-Sixteenth Century:** woman

a Gown worn over underdress, with strongly stiffened, long-waisted bodice, and full-gathered skirt, open at front to show underskirt; the open sleeve shows undersleeve; possibly of satin or taffeta.

b Padded roll, worn below the waist and under the skirt to hold out the hips and back of the full skirt.

c Shaped waistband to skirt and underskirt; a petticoat is needed with, preferably, a narrow padded roll at the floor hem.

d Stomacher (front panel of bodice), very long and pointed, strongly canvassed and boned to keep it absolutely rigid.

e Iron corset, as worn by Queen Elizabeth I.

f Felt hat with feathers; double organdie collar with lace border.

g Black felt hat, worn by tradesman's wives. See Fig. 20 for method of making ruff.

FIG 22   **End of the Seventeenth to Mid-Eighteenth Century**: man

a The coat is a much slimmer version of the one described in Fig. 24; its pleating is at the side which is left opened or sometimes buttoned; the breeches are cut according to the pattern of Fig. 24.

b Cutting pattern for coat and sleeve.

c Coat buttoned and worn with sash low on the hip.

d Black felt three-cornered hat with feathers.

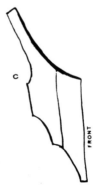

**FIG 23   Mid-Seventeenth to Early
Eighteenth Century:**
woman

a Overdress looped back to show
underskirt; bodice strongly
stiffened and boned, worn over
corset.

b Back of overdress.

c Cutting pattern of bodice.

d Fontange head-dress made of
stiffened, pleated lace——or from
nylon horsehair.

e Eighteenth-century corset.

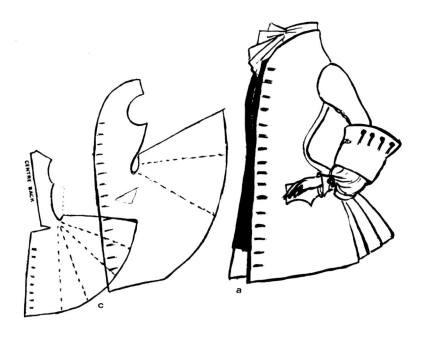

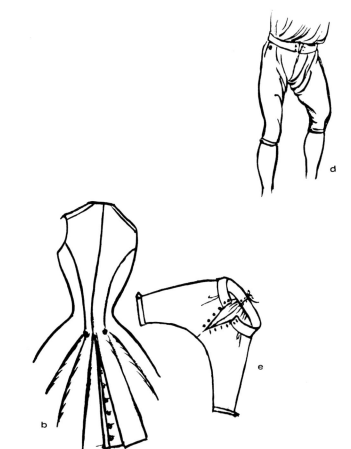

FIG 24 **Eighteenth Century:** man

a and **b** Very full-skirted collarless coat; it is important to make the back seams narrow towards a low waist.

c Many flared pieces are necessary to make the full-pleated coat-tail.

d and **e** Breeches were cut with a full-gathered seat and very low waistband. This cut gives a close-fitting leg and plenty of freedom to sit and move.

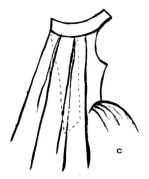

FIG 25 **Mid-Eighteenth Century:** woman

a The watteau back was cut all in one with the fitted boned bodice (**b**) and was not a separate piece attached.

c It is possibly easier to make a linen or canvas back to the under-bodice—see dotted line; cut a very wide flared back, and box-pleat this into the shaped neckband.

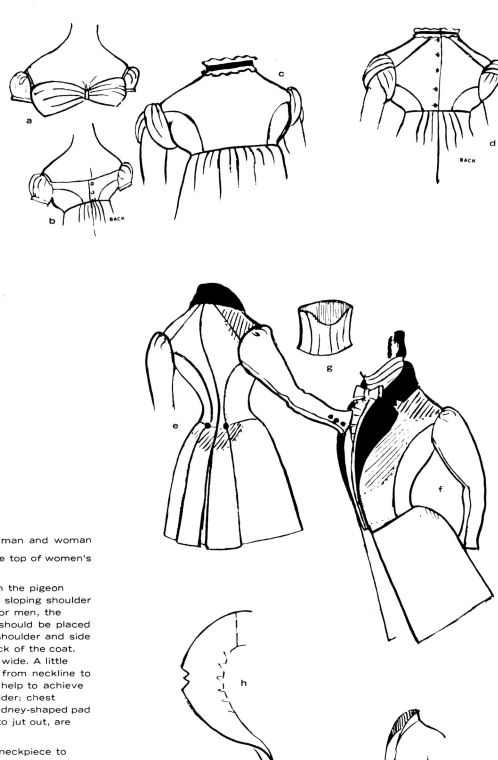

FIG 26   1812: man and woman

a, b, c and **d** The top of women's dresses.

e and **f** To attain the pigeon pouter chest and sloping shoulder then in fashion for men, the shoulder seams should be placed well behind the shoulder and side seams at the back of the coat. Cut the shoulder wide. A little 'graded' padding from neckline to sleeve head will help to achieve the sloping shoulder; chest padding, and a kidney-shaped pad to help the seat to jut out, are also advisable.

g Canvas fitted neckpiece to mount the stock.

h and **i** If a very high collar is needed, it may be worth adding a stand collar-band to the coat and fixing collar and revers to that.

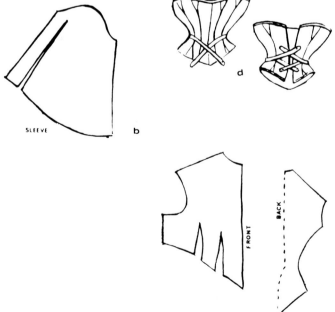

FIG 27   **Mid-Nineteenth Century:**
woman

a Dress worn over crinoline and
many frilled petticoats; the bodice
has an open-fronted sleeve
(showing the very full muslin
blouse sleeve beneath), is cut
with a pointed waist front and
will need boning.

b Pattern for cutting bodice with
long shoulder seam, to make for
'drooping' shoulder line.

c Crinoline made of strong
unbleached calico, with shaped
waistband, buttoned front and
crinoline steels.

d Corsets of the period.

e Back of bonnet.

f Muslin collar.

FIG 28 **1908**: woman's coat

a Completed coat.

b The placing of the seams.

c A cutting pattern for the coat.

d Cutting pattern for bell-topped sleeve.

9: THE BASIC COSTUME

A permanent wardrobe of 'basic costumes' for an amateur or professional company wanting to produce plays in period dress, is an invaluable asset, achieving an 'indication' of period often much more successful than detailed historic reproduction of period dress.

The basic costume can consist, for male actors, of wool tights and a cloth jacket or thick button-through wool cardigan; and for women, of several half circular ground-length skirts, a fitted cloth jacket or button-through wool cardigan. The skirts should have a draw tape round the waist, the tapes being brought out through a hole in the centre of the waist band (see FIG. 30), and press studs or velcro down the open side. They can be worn singly, or several can be fastened together with the press studs; two, three or four pulled up tight to the waist with the draw tapes will make a very full skirt. Full calico petticoats will also be needed.

The skirts will also make good cloaks for men or women. Experiments with such additions as sleeves, epaulets, sashes, garters, belts, beads and appliqués (and the right sort of hat and foot-wear) will prove that an enormous variety of costumes is possible.

FIG 29   **Basic Costume for Men**

a Basic jacket or wool cardigan.

b Basic wool tights.

c Medieval: add sleeves, hat, belt and shoes.

d Eighteenth century: add sleeveless waistcoat (see cutting pattern for eighteenth-century coat), cuffs with bag sleeves and frills attached, neckband and jabot, garters and shoes.

e Elizabethan: add ruff and cuff ruffs, epaulets and sleeves, padded hip roll, garters; trim with wool braid.

f Jacobean: add collar and cuffs with 'Vandyked' borders, wide sash with peplum, boots with turn-down tops, big felt hat with feathers (you can make very good ostrich feathers of slittered tarlatan mounted on a flat hat wire); use basic skirt as cloak.

g Peasant: leave basic jacket unbuttoned; push up sleeves; add necktie or bandana handkerchief, shirt, belt, thick wool stockings or wool tights worn over basic tights, felt boots.

h Nineteenth century: add high-shaped neckband and stock, velvet cuffs with frills attached, leather belt with coat-tails and striped waistcoat, riding boots.

i Basic skirt used as medieval cloak.

110

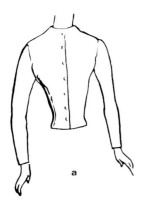

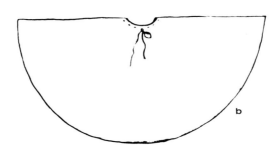

FIG 30　Basic Costume for Women

a Basic jacket or wool cardigan.

b Half-circular skirt, with draw tape and snaps.

c Peasant: leave jacket unbuttoned over low-necked sleeveless blouse; add bead necklace, wide wool jersey sash; use three half-circular skirts, attached with snaps together and gathered up with draw tapes, over calico petticoat.

d Nineteenth century: basic jacket; add frills, a bustle drape, use two half-circular skirts, one gathered on a tape and placed at the back over a bustle pad.

e Victorian: basic tops with neck turned in to form a V; add velvet braid, muslin neckpiece with a neck frill and cameo, shaped velvet waist belt, velvet cuffs; use four skirts, worn over several calico petticoats.

f Medieval: basic top and one half-circular skirt; padded rolls at neck and hip line; add sleeves and head-dress.

g Another kind of medieval sleeve.

h Eighteenth century: bone top with stitched-in neck line; add frill and bow, cuffs with bag sleeve and frills attached; use two half-circular skirts worn over calico petticoat; another skirt looped up for panniers.

i Elizabethan: basic top with braid trimming; add sleeves and padded hip roll, calico petticoats, calico panel with applique: use four basic skirts left unfastened in front to show panel.

[77]

PLATE 77 MOTLEY

Dancers in **Kwamina,** choreography by
Agnes DeMille in 1961. These costumes
are nothing more than cotton mu mus over
cotton skirts.

'JACKIE' ACT II
LYNN REDGRAVE
EVENING

PLATES 78 & 79
MOTLEY

Jackie Coryton (Lynn
Redgrave) and Judith
Bliss (Edith Evans) in
Hay Fever, directed
by Noel Coward in
1964. As the play is
naturalistic these are
fairly close
representations of
dress in the 1920s.

[78]

EDITH EVANS.
JUDITH BLISS
BREAKFAST. ACT III
VELVET. WITH LACE & CHIFF.

8 yds velvet
8 yds linin.
4 yds. slip
1½ shurf

MOTLEY - 64

[79]

ACT II Sc. 2
Brighton Pavillion
the Prince[?]
Coronation Robe

[81]

PLATE 80

The Regent (Walter Slezak) in **The First Gentleman,** directed by Tyrone Guthrie in 1957. Collection, Mr. and Mrs. Alexander H. Cohen. The Regent's trousers were made of an eggshell 'elastique.' He wore a lilac and eggshell vest, and his various decorations and orders were made of braid pearls and jewels.

PLATE 81

The Regent (Walter Slezak), Princess Charlotte (Inga Swenson), and Leopold in **The First Gentleman,** directed by Tyrone Guthrie in 1957. Photo, Eileen Darby, Graphic House. In this scene, the Regent wore a vest which was embroidered in straw braid pearls, jewels, and large oval sequins mounted on gold net.

PLATE 82   ANN ROTH

Apothecary (Dennis Jones) in **Romeo and Juliet,** directed by Allen Fletcher in 1965 at the American Shakespeare Festival Theatre, Stratford.

PLATE 83   ANN ROTH

Juliet (Maria Tucci) in **Romeo and Juliet,** directed by Allen Fletcher in 1965 at the American Shakespeare Festival Theatre, Stratford.

PLATE 84
ANN ROTH

Prince Escalus and
attendants in **Romeo
and Juliet,** directed by
Allen Fletcher in 1965
at the American
Shakespeare Festival
Theatre, Stratford.

[84]

[85]

[86]

PLATE 85   MOTLEY

Drinkers in **King Henry IV**, directed by Douglas Seale in 1962 at the American Shakespeare Festival Theatre, Stratford. These costumes were made of rough wools and furnishing fabrics of various textures. The men wore heavy wool tights and soft suede and leather shoes.

PLATE 86   MOTLEY

Two women in **King Henry IV**, directed by Douglas Seale in 1962 at the American Shakespeare Festival Theatre, Stratford. Here the women wore rough wools of various textures, some furnishing materials, and soft suede shoes.

PLATE 87   MOTLEY

The Vintner in **King Henry IV**, directed by Douglas Seale in 1962 at the American Shakespeare Festival Theatre, Stratford.

[87]

[88]

PLATE 88   MOTLEY

Puritans in **Simon Boccanegra,** a
Metropolitan Opera production staged by
Margaret Webster in 1960. These
costumes were made of rough wools, raw
silks, and cottons sprayed and dyed
to give an aged look. The puritans wore
wool tights and shabby suede shoes.

[89]

[90]

PLATE 89   MOTLEY

Three soldiers in **Mother Courage**,
directed by Jerome Robbins in 1963.
The soldiers were dressed in pieces
of armour over army jackets, wool
trousers, and old leather boots.

PLATE 90   MOTLEY

Peasant boy in **Mother Courage**, directed
by Jerome Robbins in 1963.

PLATE 91   MOTLEY

Man with patch in **Mother Courage**,
directed by Jerome Robbins in 1963.

[91]

[2]

[93]

PLATE 92   MOTLEY

The old colonel in **Mother Courage**, directed by Jerome Robbins in 1963.

PLATE 93

The chaplain in **Mother Courage**, directed by Jerome Robbins in 1963.

PLATE 94 MOTLEY

Don Quixote
(Fernandel), designed
for Michael Todd's
birthday celebration
in Madison Square
Garden, New York,
1957.

PLATE 95 MOTLEY

Design for Elizabeth
Taylor's wool jersey
costume worn at
Michael Todd's
birthday celebration
in Madison Square
Garden, New York,
1957.

[94]   [95]

[96]

[97]

PLATE 96 MOTLEY

Two musicians in **Ben Franklin in Paris**, directed by Michael Kidd in 1964. The color scheme of these costumes consisted of indigo blues, dull reds, eggshell, taupe, and olive.

PLATE 97 MOTLEY

Dr. Caius (Morris Carnovsky) in **Merry Wives of Windsor**, directed by John Houseman and Jack Landau in 1959 at the American Shakespeare Festival Theatre, Stratford.

PLATE 98 MOTLEY

Three men in **Merry Wives of Windsor**, directed by John Houseman and Jack Landau in 1959 at the American Shakespeare Festival Theatre, Stratford.

[98]

127

[99]

PLATE 99   MOTLEY

The Doge (Leonard Warren) in **Simon Boccanegra**,
a Metropolitan Opera production staged by
Margaret Webster in 1960. The Doge's cape was made
of a cream velvet applique on gold with gold tassels.
His robe was made of gold and lacquer red
hand-painted linen.

10: THE INFLUENCE OF HISTORY AND ARCHITECTURE

The costume designer is irrevocably linked to the past as well as the present, and influenced as much by history as he is by the events of the contemporary scene. He is well advised to study the history of dress and architecture in order to understand what these influences are. A designer may have talent and imagination in abundance, but these gifts will not entirely compensate for lack of knowledge. It is doubtful if even a genius will go very far along the way ahead if he is completely ignorant of the road behind.

FIRST GARMENTS From earliest times, man has influenced dress and building, and they have influenced him. The first garments and habitations made by human hands must have been motivated by the need for protection from other men and animals and for shelter from excessive heat or cold. Primitive tribesmen erected stockaded villages, then rough fortresses, then walled towns; and it was natural that they should fashion garments in the crude image of the place that gave them sustenance and security.

TYRANNIES OF FASHION There are critics of modern life who firmly aver that the great political and economic despotisms of the past have only given way to a number of smaller but ugly tyrannies in the present – including a tyranny of fashion. But, whether present modes represent an artistic ascent into the stratosphere, so to speak, or the ultimate down-curve of a dismal trajectory, the designer must deal with them; they are, for better or worse, a part of the evolution of his craft. They are also a part of history, a long history that offers, to the student of visual objects, perhaps more lessons than it does to any other man.

Playwrights may occasionally devise scripts laid in such unlikely locales as the morning before Genesis, the day after Eternity, or the amorphous regions of outer space; but such offerings will be rare, and only imagination can help bring them to life. For the most part, the designer works with subjects more or less deeply rooted in historical reality, and although his stock-in-trade may be illusion, he must also deal in the staples of unlovely fact. If he thoroughly understands what forces combined to make some of his materials no better than they should be, he may be the fortunate designer who can manage always to make them appear a little better than they are.

129

FIG 31
Egyptian

EGYPT   If the early shelters and clothing reflected man's savage will to survive, the edifices and costumes of ancient Egypt showed a very different attitude. The pharaohs, obsessed with thoughts of death, turned the Nile valley into a vast royal cemetery, and the harsh angularity of the great tombs permeated every aspect of Egyptian art, culture and daily life. Temples and palaces, head-dresses, the costumes of priest and dancer, slave and soldier, all reflected the bleak preoccupations of the pharaohs with their mausoleums.

FIG 32
Greek

FIG 33
Roman

ROME   Egyptian costume is, perhaps, the classic example of the influence of architecture upon clothing. Yet the more liberal Greeks and Romans were almost as diligent in pursuing a certain uniformity in building and personal dress. We may need greater visual subtlety to realize it, but the connection between them was certainly there. The folds of cloth fell as straight as plumb-lines, as nearly precipitately vertical as the clean, straight columns that were lifted from the earth. Even when it attempted to be casual, Greek and Roman dress held a sense of order and discipline, a quality almost as functional and antiseptic as the shapes and colours of their villas and temples and baths.

FIG 34
The Dark Ages

THE DARK AGES   The so-called Dark Ages were almost formless in their architecture and costume; those were indeed years of iron and stone, and of iron and stone mentalities. With the exception of peasant hutments, fortress-castles and war machines, most of the building was done by the Church, and most clothing was still extemporized from whatever came to hand. Some of the church architecture was beautiful, and the effulgence of the great edifices was echoed in the garments of wealthy nobles, who appreciated rich colour and rich cloth. But the peacocks were few and the sparrows many, and man in general was a wretched and shabby creature who seemed to have lost his capacity both to imitate and to invent.

FIG 35
The Middle Ages

FIG 36
'Decorated'

THE MIDDLE AGES The awakening, of course, was spectacular. In the Middle Ages man's imagination soared to new heights in building and in dress. The tall spires, pointed arches and comparatively simple columns were echoed in the long lines of the gowns and hanging sleeves, and the plain outline of the figure. And as gothic architecture progressed from the relative simplicity of the 'Early English' style to the elaboration of the 'Decorated', with its abundant carving and more complex tracery, costume followed suit.

FIG 37
Tudor and Elizabethan

TUDOR ENGLAND   History has been lavish in presenting us with examples of man's susceptibility to environment, and there is also ample evidence that environment was highly susceptible to him. Few figures celebrated in history are more familiar to laymen than England's King Henry VIII. Most of us recognize immediately any portrayal of the burly monarch in his heavy, square-cut court dress. But in considering Henry's more spectacular exploits, we are inclined to overlook the great influence which he exerted upon the building of the day, and the influence which that same building exerted upon the king himself.

Henry Tudor gave his name to a new and revolutionary period in English architecture, and in turn the period gave his son Henry the bulky clothing that he wore. Certainly there is more than coincidence in the fact that the figure of this hulking royal giant, seen in silhouette, fits almost perfectly into the sturdy outlines of a Tudor arch. All things were so far as was possible in Bluff Hal's image: castles and cannons, the clothes of courtiers, a new concept in public housing, for example.

FIG 38
Seventeenth century

THE ELIZABETHANS   Throughout this period and the Elizabethan one which followed it, the human body became more and more distorted – by padding, by enormous quantities of heavy material and by elaborate decoration and detail. The Tudor forms were simple and broad, but the architecture, furniture and dress of the Elizabethans was bulbous and extremely stiff.

SEVENTEENTH CENTURY   The seventeenth century brought a reaction. For a time the shape of figures became more natural and less exaggerated. Then fashion dictated exaggeration once again – but this time in the opposite direction; everything had to be tall and narrow – windows, furniture, hair styles, and head-dresses.

FIG 39
Eighteenth century

EIGHTEENTH
CENTURY   In the eighteenth century the connection between the various branches became
much less clear, though it can still be seen in some details and in the general attitude
to design. The common denominator seems to be a simple broad outline with elaborate
decoration within it.

FIG 40
Nineteenth century: Regency and Victorian

**REGENCY AND
VICTORIAN ERAS**

After this time, fashion in dress began to change so rapidly that it is very difficult to see a clear parallel with architecture. The Regency period stressed simple classical lines and geometric patterns and details. But the Victorian ran riot with complicated shapes and forms, based on styles from all the great periods; these were often mixed on the same piece of architecture or furniture, and one costume might have many different types of decoration and trimming.

11: SOME THOUGHTS IN CLOSING

The points we have touched on in the preceding chapters are, in the final analysis, largely theoretical. There are, of course, some arbitrary rules, but most of them are open to individual interpretation. Every aspect of costume design *must* necessarily stem from the initial desire to create something original, whether it be a new interpretation of clothes of a past era or a novel adaptation of contemporary dress. Once the fundamentals of draftsmanship and historical orientation have been mastered, the student or beginner may learn more from the experience of one actual production than may be gleaned from an entire encyclopedia of costume design; that is to say, he may learn more about himself in relation to the art of costume design. He will, we hope, finally enjoy the realization that his inspiration holds validity on the stage. There can be no yardstick for creativity of this sort, unless one considers the human eye as such, and the human eye can be no less individual than the human mind through which it functions.

Rules are, nevertheless, necessary even for the most exalted theorists, and in view of their importance, it would be well to summarize them here.

THE IMPORTANCE OF RESEARCH Proper research is the primary essential for attempting to interpret any period. Whenever possible, one should use the *paintings* of contemporaries of a particular period, rather than merely refer to pictures of costumes of the period. One of the sources to which we have referred is *The Book of Costume*, by Millia Davenport,* which has an excellent text and hundreds of reproductions of drawings and paintings of the various periods. There are few exceptions to the above rule, but we have often allowed ourselves reference to *Costume Cavalcade* by Harald Hansen, Methuen, London, which contains 685 examples of historic costume in colour. These drawings clearly show the changes in costume silhouette from one era to the next. Museums and galleries should be visited and revisited as often as possible, for it is fair to assume that no one's research is ever really completed or that it can be over-done. It is well worth making a personal collection of any photographs, reproductions, advertisements, postcards and so on which might be interesting or useful, and evolving a good filing system for them, so what is needed can easily be found, and to make sketches or take photographs of anything you come across which you think helpful and add it to this collection.

DRAFTSMANSHIP Draftsmanship is, quite naturally, a necessary rudiment for imparting your ideas and creations to the director and the costumier, but it must necessarily follow that the designer should fully understand how the clothes of every period are made – from the standpoint of cut, the placement of seams, the sewing and fastening, and other details necessary to achieve the desired ultimate effect.

* Crown Publishers, New York

USING COLOUR   Understanding colour and knowing how to use it is one matter of great importance, but it is quite separate from the matter of the effect of stage lighting on colour. The likelihood that a designer will become familiar with stage directions and theatrical parlance does not mean that he will have to become proficient in the ways of technical stage lighting, but he should be able to call for what he wants in the way of lighting to achieve the desired effect. As we have pointed out, designers may be fortunate enough in some instances to have a preview of the lighting plot or to discuss their problems with the lighting expert, and perhaps even turn a spot light on their colours and study the effects.

CHARACTER DELINEATION   Apart from extraordinary instances, such as dressing the chorus of some operatic or musical productions, the designer must conceive and draw and later help to unfold an image which clearly *delineates character*; so that this character is revealed as much by the costume as by the dialogue of the play and the performance of the actor.

TEMPERAMENTAL CONSIDERATIONS   What is the required temperament? The designer who has endured through more than a few successful productions may be said to have the qualities needed. We have said earlier that he must not be faint of heart, but no summary of his requirements could be finished without re-emphasizing the demands that this profession will make on his health, his stamina and his spirit. He should have the skin of the proverbial rhinoceros, the heart of a lion and the tenacity of a bull-dog. Ideally, all these attributes will be combined with a rare form of spirit, common to those only who belong to a special and rather peculiar breed of man. Temperament such as this cannot be devoid of certain dark moments – periods of exasperation, frustration, possibly even despair. The opposition to one's principles, the obstacles preventing an exact execution of one's designs, schedules and meetings that seem to interfere with one's work, difficult dealings with performers, struggling to come to a *complete* understanding with the director, are just a few of the problems likely to be encountered in this rather unlikely profession.

The demands made of him are widely varied and often unique, yet the final rewards are eminently satisfactory. If they were not, this book would not have been written.

SELECT BIBLIOGRAPHY

Arnold, Janet, PATTERNS OF FASHION 1660–1860 (Macmillan, London, 1972)
—— PATTERNS OF FASHION 1860–1940 (Macmillan, London, 1972)

Barton, Lucy, HISTORIC COSTUME FOR THE STAGE (A&C Black, London, 1961 and W. H. Baker, Boston, 1963)
Boehn, Max von, DIE MODE (Bruckman, Munich, 9 vols, 1909). English edition (translated by Joan Joshua), MODES AND MANNERS including a volume on ornaments (Harrap, London, 1935)
Boucher, François, 20,000 YEARS OF FASHION (Harry N. Abrams, New York, 1987) and as A HISTORY OF COSTUME IN THE WEST (Thames and Hudson, London, 1988)

Cunnington, C. W., A DICTIONARY OF ENGLISH COSTUME 900–1900 (A&C Black, London, 1960)
—— A PICTURE HISTORY OF ENGLISH COSTUME (The Studio, London and Macmillan, New York, 1950)
Cunnington, C. W. and Phillis, A HANDBOOK OF ENGLISH MEDIAEVAL COSTUME (Faber, London, 1972)
—— A HANDBOOK OF ENGLISH COSTUME IN THE SIXTEENTH CENTURY (Faber, London and Plays Inc. Boston, 1970)
—— A HANDBOOK OF ENGLISH COSTUME IN THE SEVENTEENTH CENTURY (Faber, London and Plays Inc. Boston, 1973)
—— A HANDBOOK OF ENGLISH COSTUME IN THE EIGHTEENTH CENTURY (Faber, London and Plays Inc., Boston, 1972)
—— A HANDBOOK OF ENGLISH COSTUME IN THE NINETEENTH CENTURY (Faber, London and Plays Inc., Boston, 1970)
Cunnington, Phillis and Lucas, Catherine, OCCUPATIONAL COSTUME IN ENGLAND FROM THE ELEVENTH CENTURY TO 1914 (A&C Black, London, 1967 and Humanities Press, Atlantic Highlands, N.J., 1976)
Cunnington, Phillis and Mansfield, Ann, A HANDBOOK OF ENGLISH COSTUME IN THE TWENTIETH CENTURY (Faber, London and Plays Inc., Boston, 1970)
Cunnington, Phillis, COSTUME IN PICTURES (revised edn Herbert Press, London, 1981), distributed in USA by Universe Books

Damase, Jacques, FASHION AND FABRICS (Thames and Hudson, London, 1991)
Davenport, Millia, THE BOOK OF COSTUME (Crown Publishers, New York, 1976)
DeMarly, Diana, WORKING DRESS: A HISTORY OF OCCUPATIONAL CLOTHING (B. T. Batsford, London, 1986)

Ewing, Elizabeth, EVERYDAY DRESS 1650–1900 (B. T. Batsford, London, 1984)
—— DRESS AND UNDRESS: A HISTORY OF WOMEN'S UNDERWEAR (B. T. Batsford, London, 1977 and Drama Book Specialists, New York, 1978)

Glynn, Prudence and Ginsburg, Madeleine, IN FASHION: DRESS IN THE TWENTIETH CENTURY (Allen & Unwin, London and Oxford University Press, New York, 1978)

Hartley, Dorothy and Elliot, Margaret, LIFE AND WORK OF THE PEOPLE OF ENGLAND (B. T. Batsford, London, 1926)
Hiler, Hilaire and Meyer, BIBLIOGRAPHY OF COSTUME (H. W. Wilson Co., New York, 1967)

Kelly, Francis M., SHAKESPEAREAN COSTUMES FOR STAGE AND SCREEN (A&C Black, London, 1938)
Kohler, Karl, A HISTORY OF COSTUME (Dover, New York and Constable & Co., London, 1963)

Jackson, Sheila, COSTUMES FOR THE STAGE (Herbert Press, London and New Amsterdam Books, New York, 1988)

Laver, James, A CONCISE HISTORY OF COSTUME (Thames and Hudson, London, 1969 and Scribner, New York, 1974)
—— THE CONCISE HISTORY OF COSTUME AND FASHION (Harry N. Abrams, New York, 1969) and as COSTUME AND FASHION, A CONCISE HISTORY (Thames and Hudson, London, 1979)

Linthicum, Marie Channing, COSTUMES IN ELIZABETHAN DRAMA (Clarendon Press, Oxford) and as COSTUME IN THE DRAMA OF SHAKESPEARE AND HIS CONTEMPORARIES (Russell and Russell, New York, 1963)

Moore, Doris Langley, FASHION THROUGH FASHION PLATES 1770–1970 (Ward Lock, London, 1971 and Potter, New York, 1972)

Morse, Harriet Klamroth, ELIZABETHAN PAGEANTRY (The Studio, London and New York, 1934)

Nunn, Joan, FASHION IN COSTUME 1200–1980 (Herbert Press, London and New Amsterdam Books, New York, 1990)

O'Hara, Georgina, ENCYCLOPEDIA OF FASHION (Thames and Hudson, 1989)

Payne, Blanche, HISTORY OF COSTUME FROM THE ANCIENT EGYPTIANS TO THE TWENTIETH CENTURY (Harper & Row, New York and London, 1965)

Tilke, Max, COSTUME PATTERNS AND DESIGNS: A SURVEY OF COSTUME PATTERNS AND DESIGNS OF ALL PERIODS AND NATIONS FROM ANTIQUITY TO MODERN TIMES (Zwemmer, London 1956 and Frederick A. Praeger, New York, 1967)

Waugh, Norah, CORSETS AND CRINOLINES (B. T. Batsford, London and Theatre Arts Books, New York, 1970)
—— THE CUT OF MEN'S CLOTHES 1600–1914 (Faber, London and Theatre Arts Books, New York, 1977)
—— THE CUT OF WOMEN'S CLOTHES 1600–1930 (Faber, London and Theatre Arts Books, New York, 1968)

Wilcox, Ruth Turner, THE DICTIONARY OF COSTUME (B. T. Batsford, London, 1971 and Scribner, New York, 1969)
—— FIVE CENTURIES OF AMERICAN COSTUME (A&C Black, London, 1966 and Scribner, New York, 1963)

Yarwood, Doreen, ENCYCLOPEDIA OF WORLD COSTUME (B. T. Batsford, London and Scribner, New York, 1978)

FABRIC INDEX

CAROLINE

QUEEN ANNE

REGENCY

MID 18th CENTURY

SILHOUETTES OF
COSTUME FROM THE 17th
TO THE 19th CENTURY

VICTORIAN

1890s

1880s

INDEX

Numbers in bold refer to captions.